'Plenty of amusing anecdotes . . . highly readable . . . the former referee's new autobiography is required reading and lays bare some of the more disturbing aspects of modern rugby'

Guardian

'Difficult to put down . . . enjoyable and thought-provoking in equal measure'

Planet Rugby

T0271703

Wayne Barnes is an English international rugby union referee and criminal barrister. He has refereed more international matches than anyone else in the history of the sport. He has refereed in five Rugby World Cups, seventeen Six Nations tournaments and three European Champions Cup finals. He has not only refereed over 270 English Premiership matches, including ten finals, but he has done so while also being a partner at the international law firm, Squire Patton Boggs.

THROWING THE BOOK

The Strife and Crimes of a
Rugby Referee

Wayne Barnes
With Ben Dirs

CONSTABLE

CONSTABLE

First published in Great Britain in 2023 by Constable
This paperback edition published in 2024 by Constable

3 5 7 9 10 8 6 4

A CIP catalogue record for this book
is available from the British Library.

ISBN: 978-1-40871-955-8

Typeset in Bembo Std by SX Composing DTP, Rayleigh, Essex
Printed and bound in Great Britain by Clays Ltd, Elcograf, S.p.A.

Papers used by Constable are from well-managed forests
and other responsible sources.

MIX
Paper | Supporting
responsible forestry
FSC® C104740

Constable
An imprint of
Little, Brown Book Group
Carmelite House
50 Victoria Embankment
London EC4Y 0DZ

The authorised representative
in the EEA is
Hachette Ireland
8 Castlecourt Centre
Dublin 15, D15 XTP3, Ireland
(email: info@hbgi.ie)

An Hachette UK Company

www.hachette.co.uk

www.littlebrown.co.uk

For Juno and Beau, who had to sacrifice their
Dad being away.

And for Polly, who has sacrificed more than anyone.
You are an inspiration to our children. You have been my
biggest fan. You always have my back. You have made me
a better person.

I love you all more than you can imagine and cannot wait
for the new chapter of our lives together.

Contents

Prologue

Someone told me I was shit at my job the other day. I'd never met him before, complete stranger. I was having a coffee at the time, minding my own business – as much as you can mind your own business when you're a rugby referee.

I suppose it was better than being wished a slow and painful death, which happens occasionally. Or someone calling me the third most evil man in the world, just behind Saddam Hussein and Osama bin Laden, because I failed to spot a forward pass. (Given that Saddam and Osama are both dead now, does that mean I'm now the most evil?) Come to think of it, maybe I should have thanked the stranger in the coffee shop for being so measured in his criticism.

I don't mind a bit of piss-taking if it's done in the right spirit, it's all that death stuff that stings a bit. I'm just a bloke trying my best, and rugby isn't the simplest of games to referee. I'd love to see some of my harshest critics try it.

When I was growing up, I didn't dream of being unpopular. Never did I say, 'You know what? I'll make it a double whammy and become a lawyer *and* a referee – so that people think I'm really, *really* awful.' It just kind of happened. But as I'm sometimes reminded, they were my choices, so I can't complain too much. And joking aside, what a wonderful life refereeing and lawyering have given me.

Like any young rugby fan, I wanted to play the game for a living, but I suffered from a severe lack of talent. However, I think I've got the next best job. I get to stand in the middle of a packed stadium, listening to some of the best rugby players in the world belt out their national anthems while trembling and crying. Then when I blow my whistle, I've got a ringside seat for eighty minutes of organised mayhem. Or one hundred minutes, but I'll return to that later.

Sometimes, I'll think to myself, *How on earth did I end up here?* In fact, that's been one of the themes of my life. A kid from Bream in the Forest of Dean, with a West Country burr so thick you could spread it on toast, isn't meant to referee at Twickenham or Murrayfield. He isn't meant to be a barrister in a wig and gown, advocating in a courtroom. He isn't meant to meet the Queen at Buckingham Palace. And he isn't meant to write books. If 'fish out of water' were a career choice, I reckon I'd have nailed it.

It's a weird occupation, refereeing. You upset a lot of people and get shouted at quite often. You're mainly remembered for the mistakes you make. If nobody is talking about you, that probably means you've done a good job. But weird as it is, I'm honestly quite normal. Well, I would say that, but you can make your own minds up. Everyone ready? Let's get things under way.

1

When I Grow Up

An Irish journalist described me as 'a deranged Eton headmaster with a ferret down his pants'. I've no idea what the ferret reference was about, but I assume by 'Eton headmaster' he was attempting to portray me as a stereotypical English rugger bloke: superior, posh, from somewhere in the Home Counties.

He couldn't have been much further from the truth. The fact I'm called Wayne should have been a clue. Believe it or not, my brother's called Darren.

To those who have never visited, the Forest of Dean probably sounds idyllic. It's true, some of the countryside down there is magnificent, but it's also quite a poor area. Once upon a time, most of the men worked in coal mining but, by the time I came along, all the collieries were long gone.

When people ask me what the Forest of Dean is like, I usually say, 'Wales.' Because besides its mining heritage, it's also got sheep, brass bands, male voice choirs – and rugby.

I was born and raised on a council estate in the village of Bream, which is only about twenty miles from Newport. And like most boys from Bream, I was turning out for the local rugby team, Bream RFC, from the age of six or seven.

Bream had two pitches, which were built on a hill. The club got some money to flatten one of them, and the committee chose the pitch at the bottom of the hill. It was constantly flooded because the top one was still sloping and rainwater ran down it. I can still smell the horrible yellow clay, which stuck to your hair and was impossible to wash out of your kit.

The changing rooms were old school, with big communal baths. On match day, there would be a chap on the gate, charging 50p to watch the game. There were plenty of eccentrics around the place, including the sponge man Lindsay, who would turn up on his clapped-out 50cc moped wearing a deerstalker.

I don't suppose Lindsay had ever done a first-aid course, and he probably did more harm than good. He once strapped someone's hand up so that all his fingers were stuck together and he couldn't catch for the rest of the game.

The rugby club was everything to everybody in the village, the one constant you could always count on. If you were having a hard time at home, the door would always be open, even for a bang-average player like me.

In the clubhouse after a game there would be lots of drunken singing and dancing, sometimes even nudity. And if there wasn't rugby going on, there was darts on Monday, skittles on Tuesday (which was taken as seriously as any Olympic sport), bingo on Wednesday, quoits on Thursday (which was taken almost as seriously as skittles), karaoke on Friday, and out-of-control birthday parties, raucous wedding receptions, boozy wakes and christenings on the weekend.

And if you weren't in Bream Rugby Club, you were down the road in Lydney Rugby Club, where the really big events took place, or the cricket club, which my nan ran (I'd help her bottle up and bring up the barrels before opening), or the snooker club, where my mum worked.

Bream's best players were well known in the community and often coached the kids. Before our kick-off on a Sunday morning, the first-team lads would stumble in from the night before and take us through some drills. After my game, I'd hang around the clubhouse, drinking pop, eating crisps, playing pool and mingling with the various club characters, some of whom virtually lived there. And at two in the afternoon, I'd wander down to my nan's club and help her tidy up, before heading home for lunch.

When I was fifteen, I got injured on the rugby field and couldn't play for a few months. While I was recovering, one of my teachers, Mr Wilkins, suggested I give refereeing a go. My first reaction was, 'Who wants to be a referee?' Then when I went to watch Bream play local rivals Berry Hill, my dad's mate Geoff, who had been a referee for years, said to me, 'The thirds don't have a ref. Mr Wilkins tells me you're doing a course. Now's your chance to see if you're any good at it.'

I told Geoff I hadn't actually started doing a course; that I didn't know the laws that well; that some of these blokes were more than twice my age. But my protests fell on deaf ears. Geoff lobbed me some boots, wished me luck and muttered something about paying me a fiver. Every cloud – for a fifteen-year-old boy in Bream in the mid-1990s, a fiver was the stuff of a madman's dreams.

A few minutes later, I was walking out to referee Bream Third XV versus Berry Hill Wappers. My boots, which were three sizes too big, were flapping in the yellow-clay mud, and I was filled with a terrible mixture of dread and excitement.

In theory, I was in charge of club stalwarts like Pete Watkins, our twenty-stone fly-half, who had been coaching me since I was six. In reality, I was in charge of no one. When I blew the whistle that Geoff had lent me, all hell broke loose. High tackles, stamping, punches. I was wandering around the pitch, not knowing where to stand or what was going on, while thirty blokes told me how to do my job. The only reason I wasn't getting a barrage of abuse was because my grandad and his mates were threatening people from the touchline.

Ten minutes in, all excitement had left me and only dread remained. One of our props, a brute of a man, told me that if I didn't stop his opposite number cheating, he'd do it instead. I asked him not to, and thought I'd done it nicely, but after a particularly messy ruck, his opposite number was flat on his back, his nose splattered across his face. Nothing I could do, didn't see it.

For the entire game, the Forest of Dean's finest knocked ten bells out of each other. And when I blew the final whistle, I mainly felt relief. But after I'd handed back my clown boots and had time to reflect, I realised it had been a hairy but exhilarating experience. You know the feeling you have after getting off a rollercoaster, or doing a bungee jump or a sky dive? That was me.

Back in the clubhouse, someone slipped me a fiver, gave me a tankard with 'Referee' engraved on it, and filled it to the brim with beer. I thought, *This could be the hobby for me.*

For the rest of that season, Geoff and I worked as a duo. If it was an away game, somewhere else in Gloucestershire, he'd pick me up and drive me there, which meant I could pocket the £5 travel expenses. Geoff would usually referee the first team and I'd referee one of the other matches, and then I'd get the traditional free pints.

One weekend, I took part in an exchange game, which involved four of us Gloucestershire refs driving down to Cornwall together. We stayed overnight in a little B&B and spent our £10 food allowance on a pie and pint on the seafront. That's the thing about refereeing – it let me do stuff a little bit different as a teenager, and it continued to do so until my very final tournament.

I was good at the drinking part – especially for a fifteen-year-old – not so much the refereeing. Talk about a steep learning curve. But it was a nice way to spend a Saturday afternoon and kept me out of Mum's hair.

Referees are normally older – people who have hung their boots up and want to give something back to their community – so I brought a bit of freak factor. Wherever I pitched up, people would be staring at me and whispering, 'Why is there a kid in the middle of the pitch?' But I actually think everyone behaved a bit better when I was reffing, because a grown man getting aggressive with a teenager isn't a great look. That said, some of the rugby in Gloucestershire in the 1990s was pretty ugly. If I was being generous, I'd call it agricultural. If I was being honest, I'd call it vicious.

In those early days, it was a case of just trying to get through each game without making a calamitous mistake. I never felt in control, and I wasn't exactly the proverbial swan, serene on the surface but pedalling furiously. In truth, I didn't have a clue what I was doing. I was making it up as I went along. I had to, because I didn't have any formal training. I started attending monthly meetings with the Gloucester and District Referees Society, which usually involved a short lesson for the newbies, but it was very casual. The attitude was, 'Just go out there and learn from experience.' Fair enough, it's not like rugby is complicated or anything.

Luckily, most players I reffed were very aware that I was just a kid trying to do the best I could, and that if I wasn't doing it, they might not have a game. They were also very keen to give me advice, usually while plying me with pints. I'd have just refereed Matson, whose clubhouse is at the bottom of a dry ski slope on a council estate, and some gnarled prop would shove a pint into my hand, usher me into a corner and treat me to an hour-long lecture on binding in the scrum. I'm not sure that sort of thing would have happened to an older referee, and they're some of my favourite memories from those early days.

I refereed everything that moved: Saturday morning schools, followed by afternoon men's seconds, thirds or fourths; Sunday morning under-15s or under-16s, followed by Sunday afternoon women's. My first season, I refereed 100 games, and I did about 250 during my first three years. On top of that, I must have run touch 100 times, usually in first XV cup games. Running touch was a great opportunity to watch and learn from more experienced referees, who would also take the time to give me advice in the clubhouse afterwards.

It was the best grounding a young referee could hope for, partly because there was a lot of violence. The Forest of Dean Combination Cup was particularly combustible because it meant so much to everyone involved, whether they were playing for or supporting their first, second or third team. Five or six hundred people would turn up to watch a second XV game between Newent and Drybrook, and games often got tasty. I soon learned that the best way to deal with a brawl was to blow my whistle, stand back and work out who to penalise while I was waiting for the violence to fizzle out.

It never stopped being challenging, but the dread melted away, and I particularly enjoyed the performance aspect, which reminded me of treading the boards. When I was younger, I appeared in loads of pantomimes in the church hall. The same twenty people came to watch every year, and the shows were pretty terrible, but I loved them, especially when I got to play Widow Twankey. I'm not sure where that came from – I'm pretty sure my dad didn't like dressing up as a woman. Then again, maybe he did and I just didn't know about it.

When I was thirteen, my drama teacher took us to see *Starlight Express* in London, my first and only trip to London before becoming a barrister. That trip gave me the taste for musicals and I quickly became a huge fan of *Les Misérables*. To date, I must have watched *Les Mis* about thirty times and I'd have given my right arm to appear in it.

But while my dream of treading the West End boards never materialised, I came to see the rugby pitch as a stage, with the players as actors, and me in the middle making everything work properly, applying the rules – or at least trying to – so the production looks as beautiful as possible.

Paradoxically, I also realised that if no one noticed me on the rugby pitch, I'd done okay. I'd got all the big decisions right but not been too pernickety and let the game flow. So it would be wrong to say I took to refereeing because I was a show-off (although there are plenty of people who would disagree), because the best thing that could happen would be that I'd blow the final whistle, stroll off the pitch and everyone would ignore me.

– ★ –

From the first team all the way down to the kids, Bream RFC could fight with the best of them. Or worst, whichever way you want to look at it.

When I was fifteen, I went on tour as a player to Antwerp (not exactly a rugby hotbed, but the coaches liked their strong Belgian beer and it had a thriving red-light district) and one of our games was against a French team. They were giving us the runaround, as French teams often do, and our front row decided that the only way to neutralise them was to start a twenty-nine-man punch-up. I say twenty-nine, not thirty, because I was hiding on the fringes, trying to stop it. Actually, it's not accurate to say twenty-nine either, because the coaches joined in as well.

Little has changed over the years. About ten years ago, I watched Bream play a Rugby Football Union (RFU) Intermediate Cup game they were expected to lose. Their opponents came from Devon, played some really nice rugby and were fifteen points up after about twenty minutes, when Bream's forwards decided to ramp up the physicality. And this time it wasn't the coaches joining in, it was the spectators. The referee didn't stop blowing his whistle, but the other team no longer wanted anything to do with the ball, and Bream ended up winning.

As well as Bream, I played rugby for Whitecross School, where I made a name for myself as a non-tackling back row, a rare beast indeed. Whitecross weren't as rough as Bream – you weren't really allowed to be in schools rugby – but we did have players who didn't mind smacking people.

I wasn't one of them, despite what certain people wanted to believe. Before I'd even started at Whitecross, a lot of my teachers had written me off because they assumed I'd be like my brother Darren, who'd just been expelled for throwing a desk at the deputy headmaster. All I had to do was drop a piece of litter and a teacher would say to me, 'You're just like your brother.' I'd be thinking, *It just fell out of my pocket!* That was my first big life lesson: people will judge you, even if they don't know you from Adam. Or, indeed, Darren.

I wasn't hard like Darren. I was tall and lanky with blond curtains and a rat's tail. I also wondered if Darren would come to my rescue if I was getting a kicking or join in instead. So I made the sensible decision to get my head down and live a peaceful life. To this day, I hate confrontation. If I hear raised voices, I'm out of there in a heartbeat. That might surprise people, given that I ended up being a barrister and a rugby referee, arguing and explaining for a living.

I'm a firm believer that childhood friends have just as much influence over your life as family members, perhaps even more. And I was lucky enough to have people in my school year who were as academic as they were sporty, as well as hard kids who had my back because I was in the rugby team.

When I was fourteen, one of my teachers, who was also a magistrate, invited me to watch a court proceeding. From that moment on, I wanted to be a barrister. As with the refereeing, the theatricality appealed to me. Like a rugby match, the courtroom featured a cast of actors, with the lawyers in the middle of things, trying to make sure everything didn't turn into a shitshow. I'd also heard that barristers got to wear wigs and gowns, and make grand speeches while waving their arms around. Plus, I'd watched a lot of *Kavanagh QC.*

Another of my teachers, a man called Ashley Thomas, was an old boy of Monmouth, a private school just over the Welsh border. He saw that I was flailing a little bit, struggling for direction, so he took me under his wing. And when I was fifteen, he invited me and my mum along to a Monmouth open day.

I couldn't really see the point, first because my parents couldn't afford it, second because it was extremely posh, like nothing I'd experienced before. The buildings looked medieval, the pupils looked dead smart in their blazers and ties, and they stood up when a teacher walked into a classroom, which blew my mind.

It was an alien world for a working-class kid like me, with my gelled-back curtains, an earring in my left lobe and a Forest accent as thick as treacle. My parents had separated, my mum worked in a snooker club and my dad drove lorries. Not that there's anything wrong with those jobs, but I imagined the parents of Monmouth pupils were all bank managers and doctors. But when I told Mr Thomas that I wouldn't fit in, he replied, 'That doesn't mean you shouldn't come here.'

Most of my mates left school at sixteen, and Whitecross didn't have a sixth form anyway (probably Darren's fault). I could have done my A levels at the Royal Forest of Dean college, but Mr Thomas convinced me that I'd have more chance of becoming a barrister if I got them from a school with more connections in the legal world. So Mr Thomas helped me apply for a scholarship to Monmouth and, to my surprise, they accepted me.

Before going to Monmouth, the only time I'd interacted with middle-class children was when I was a contestant on 'Run the Risk', that bit on the Saturday-morning children's TV show *Going Live!* where kids answered quiz questions, got gunged and screamed a lot. The other kids on 'Run the Risk' had names like Jemima and Oliver, and they spoke proper. I couldn't answer any of the questions, but I bided my time and wreaked havoc in the final stages, elbowing and tossing them into the gunge. Despite a hefty penalty for answering the fewest questions correctly, I came first, and my prize was a shiny new Casio keyboard, which I hugged all the way home to Bream.

The point of this detour is that, despite feeling like I didn't belong in the cutthroat world of children's television quizzing, I managed to thrive. And so it was at Monmouth.

It was in nearby Newport, at the Queen's Head Hotel, that I received my first punch in the face. When I asked my assailant why he'd punched me, he looked perplexed before replying, 'Because you're fucking English.' And while Monmouth School wasn't quite as intolerant of English people, it was an even steeper learning curve than refereeing.

For reasons I can't remember, I enrolled to do A-level physics, despite not really knowing what physics was. Then there was politics. To mark the 1997 general election, sixth formers were invited to participate in a mock election, complete with our own parties, manifestos, campaigning and hustings, before a vote at the end of it all. More because we got lessons off than any political interest, I set up the Spice Girls Party, a single-issue outfit whose sole promise was to deliver a visit from Geri Halliwell, my favourite Spice Girl.

The irony of a one-promise policy I knew I couldn't deliver, in an election I didn't think I could win, is not lost on me now. But I campaigned with vigour and won 70 per cent of the vote, to the annoyance of my teachers. Remarkably, some of the kids who voted for me thought I really would deliver Geri Halliwell, but I had about as much sympathy for them as I now have for those who thought Brexit would deliver an extra £350 million a week for the NHS.

The only other major controversy during my time at Monmouth came when I was refereeing a staff match and penalised my maths teacher Mr Bell so many times that he lost his rag and started verbally abusing me. I marched him back ten metres, which everyone apart from Mr Bell thought was hilarious. I also sent off one of my mates when Monmouth played Lydney Colts. Someone had to go, it was absolute carnage, but it didn't win me any friends.

I often think back to Mr Thomas and realise what a pivotal role he played in my life, a sliding doors moment perhaps. He saw something in me, and he was willing to go the extra mile to help me. He wasn't one of those who had written me off from the day I walked into Whitecross. Teachers can be pretty awesome, kids. He was.

— ★ —

During school holidays, I'd do shift work back in the Forest, like squashing blackcurrants at the Ribena factory in Coleford. When I wasn't squashing blackcurrants, I might be catching up with what my brother had been up to.

After getting chucked out of Whitecross, Darren was sent to a school for naughty kids in Gloucester, where it was more crowd control than teaching. He packed that up at fifteen and learned about motorbikes instead. Some days, I'd see him riding a motorbike across the school fields. He also started DJing, graduating from Bream Rugby Club to illegal raves all over the southwest. When I became a barrister, I'd get calls along the lines of, 'Mate, the farmer's trying to turn my speakers off. Can I smack him?' The answer to that question was no, but you didn't really need a law degree to know that. I'd have mates phoning me about all sorts of issues, from being evicted by their landlord to problems with their employer, and I'd have to say, 'That's not my area of expertise. If you twat someone in the pub, I might be able to help.'

Darren wasn't a bad man, he was just mischievous. We had the same sense of humour and continued to get on like a house on fire, despite being so different on the surface. He's got two grown-up kids now and is an amazing dad to them. He's got a good job doing up streetlights, he sets up fire pits at festivals, and he and his partner spend most weekends travelling around the country in their camper van. Sometimes, I look at him and think, 'He went in a completely different direction to me, but maybe he got it right.'

It was the same with lots of my old friends from Bream, blokes like Chunk, who was always in the middle of things when it kicked off on a rugby field. (If I remember rightly, it was Chunk who started the mass brawl in Belgium.) Then there was my best mate Lardy, whose dad was also called Lardy because, you won't be surprised to learn, they were both quite lardy.

The Forest is still where I feel most at home, and I'm proud to say I'm from there. It's in more refined circles, as you might call them, that I sometimes feel a bit of a fraud. But that feeling has dissipated over the years, and I think that staying true to my roots has helped, not hampered, me in my twin careers.

You meet people from all walks of life when you're a rugby referee and a barrister – powerful and famous, poor and forgotten, blue-blooded, bourgeois and salt of the earth – and you've got to be able to relate to everyone on the spectrum.

2

Giving Up the Game

I was an average student who never did work out physics. So while fellow pupils earned places at Oxford and Cambridge, I ended up at the University of East Anglia in Norwich, which is a classic clearing university, the kind of place you end up if you don't get the grades needed by Durham, Exeter or Bristol. But as it turned out, going to UEA was the best thing that could have happened.

UEA had a vibrant campus set-up, a buzzing student union bar (I probably spent more time in there during my four years at UEA than in my own bed) and a rugby club. But best of all, it was 250 miles from Bream and I could start anew. I would no longer be known as DJ Darren's kid brother or that twat who promised that Ginger Spice would visit his school.

Alas, I couldn't hide the real me for long, and within a few days of arriving, people were shouting 'Worzel' at me everywhere I went. At first, I assumed they were calling me Worzel because I dressed like Worzel Gummidge, the TV scarecrow. It was only in my second year that someone kindly pointed out that it was more to do with the fact that I sounded like him.

Mercifully, the rugby blokes who christened me Worzel were just as simple as me. The likes of Ox, Bruno, Toon, Lurch, Byker, Crack and Candle really were idiotic souls, which a Bream lad like me found comforting. The closest thing to a scholar among us was Uncle Ivan, and even he was a borderline imbecile.

Pretty much anyone who's played rugby will know the feeling of safety that comes with knowing that as sure as the sun will rise and set every day, you'll have the piss taken out of you relentlessly, and never be called by your given name again. And when your given name is Wayne, that's an added bonus.

But rugby-club piss taking isn't an end in itself, it's deeper than that, a way of signalling that when you've lost your way and need a helping hand, at least one of those mates will offer you his and pull you back again. That's why I wore the name Worzel with pride, because it meant I'd found my new tribe.

I wore several hats at university: a stupid hat while I was doing stupid university things with my stupid mates; an academic hat while I was studying law; and a referee's hat at weekends. And strange as it might sound, the stupid hat taught me quite a lot about good judgement, which is one thing every referee needs.

A good referee is one who sees something and deals with it in a way that best serves the laws, the players and the spectacle of the game. That's why it takes a long time for a referee to develop their skills. A good referee will also surround themselves with people whose opinions and expertise they can draw upon. Sometimes, those people will challenge and even criticise you, but if you welcome their views with honesty and humility, you will see things differently, almost always learn something, improve and, in turn, make better judgements.

Of course, at university it's customary to make bad judgements, because you're surrounded by people giving you the worst advice imaginable.

It was the night before UEA was due to host an annual sevens tournament and electricity was in the air. My mates and I always liked to mark the eve of the greatest day of the year by doing something so unbelievably stupid it would make our day-to-day behaviour seem sensible. Wise even.

On this occasion, we decided to set up camp on the pitch early and plan our colossal stupidity over a crate of beers. None of what happened next was big or clever, but that's what happens when you're twenty, running with a pack of fools and high on the intoxicating whiff of freedom.

Candle had the first dim idea of the evening (ironically, Candle rarely had bright ones) and, minutes later, he was manoeuvring his car on to the pitch. After driving a few lengths, Candle started to speed up, while shouting something about needing to reach 88mph in order to travel through time, like Doc Brown's DeLorean in *Back to the Future*. I'm not proud of it now, but I found it side-splittingly hilarious at the time. Until, that is, Candle lost control, and instead of his car disappearing into the future with a bolt of lightning, it rolled three or four times up a bank before finally coming to rest on its roof.

On reaching the wreck, we found Candle with his arm jammed under the car. But after lifting the car off him, he emerged unscathed, apart from dizziness and shock. There were a few seconds of collective relief that our mate was still alive and intact, followed by sheer panic. How on earth were we going to explain this? And was this the end of my dream of becoming a barrister?

The car's roof was crushed, meaning you couldn't see through the windscreen and we didn't think we'd be able to drive it off the pitch. Then someone said, 'Worz, isn't your dad a mechanic?' They were right, so I got straight on the phone to him.

'Dad,' I said, my voice trembling, 'we've rolled Candle's car and we think it's a write-off. What should we do?'

I'd like to be able to say there was a moment's pause while my dad was weighing up the options and thinking very carefully about what advice to give. In truth, his response came quick as a flash.

'Burn it,' he said.

'Hmm?' I replied.

'Burn it,' he said again, this time with a hint of threat.

I hung up.

You'll be relieved to know that we didn't torch the car in the Forest manner, although a couple of the lads were keen on the idea. Instead, we managed to manoeuvre it to the top of the university drive before legging it home and hiding.

The whole episode was a shambles, like a scene from *The Inbetweeners*. People knew we were responsible (I imagined some student sleuth, down on one knee on the touchline, examining an empty can of cider and saying, 'This can only be the work of Worzel and his crew . . .'), but we were never brought to book. And it taught me that even when things turn out bad, you can learn a lot about judgement, especially about which people to take advice from. Or not.

Another sliding doors moment, for sure. I doubt I'd have convinced many barristers' chambers to take a punt on me with an arson conviction tagged on to my degree.

When I first arrived at UEA, I was at Level 6 or 7 in refereeing terms, the Premiership being Level 1. But when I turned up at a Norfolk Referees Society meeting and volunteered to officiate some local games, the response was, 'Son, you're only eighteen. You've got to do at least five years before you can referee those kinds of games.'

I explained that I'd been refereeing in Gloucestershire since I was fifteen, which raised a few eyebrows. But they checked out my credentials, gave me a chance and I did okay.

Soon I was refereeing games all over East Anglia, and there was something romantic about heading to some obscure rural village on a train or a bus, my kit bag on my lap. It helped that I recognised the characters at each club, because they were the same type of people I grew up with.

One of the most memorable games was a second XV dust-up between Norwich and North Walsham, who were bitter rivals. When I turned up, I could see people looking at me thinking, *Who's this little weirdo?*, like people must have looked at that blond child antique dealer who used to be on TV in the eighties. But I managed to avert all-out war, got the big decisions right, and ended up getting the minibus to Norwich city centre with the North Walsham lads.

We spent all night drinking and dancing on tables, before clambering back on the minibus and riding halfway back to North Walsham, when I suddenly remembered I lived in Norwich. I finally got home at about 4 a.m.

As I moved up the levels, the games became more far-flung. Club fixture secretaries would call me and say, 'Wayne, can you come down to Broadstairs on Saturday?' I'd have to leave at six in the morning because the train journey to London took over two hours. I'd then get a tube across London before taking another hour-and-a-half train journey down to Broadstairs, where someone from the club would pick me up and ferry me to the ground.

After the game, and another colossal booze-up, I'd sleep on the captain's sofa or in the chairman's spare room, because the trains stopped running at 9 p.m. and I didn't have money for a B&B. That kind of hospitality put me

26

under extra pressure, because I worried that if I screwed over the home team, I might be sleeping at the train station, without any cans of lager for the trip home.

But a neutral referee, however well treated, always makes more sense than a local one. Later in my career, I refereed Lydney, just down the road from Bream. They were playing West Hartlepool, and neither team had won all season. With five minutes to go, Lydney were leading by two points, and the captain kept saying, 'Barnesy, just blow up. Come on, you're one of us. Blow up, blow up, blow up . . .' His attempted Jedi mind trick didn't work, but Lydney hung on for the win.

When I was able to get back to Norwich after a game, I'd turn up in the student union bar wearing my Norfolk Referees blazer, tie and badge combination. People would be downing bottles of blue WKD through a straw and necking Guinness from boots, and I looked like a young Alan Partridge.

Those refereeing days, boozy as they usually were, were welcome breaks from student life – the toil and the mayhem – and a chance to converse with and learn from sensible adults, the kind of men Bruno wasn't and never would be. Arriving back in Norwich with fifty quid travelling expenses in my pocket and a four-pack of beer in my kit bag was the cherry on top of the cake.

At Norfolk Referees Society meetings, I picked the brains of more experienced officials, to improve as a referee, but also in the hope it would give us an advantage if any of those officials ended up in charge of a big UEA game.

I also started doing some coaching for the Norfolk Referees Society, so I knew which referees were good, average or still had an awful lot to learn. I'd pass that knowledge on to my UEA teammates, so that they would go into a game knowing if they'd get away with cheating or not.

One bloke, Billy, used to referee rugby league, so he'd stand on the defensive line, facing the breakdown, shouting, 'With me! With me!' We knew if we had Billy in charge, we'd be able to stand behind him, two or three metres offside, and he wouldn't notice. Thinking about it, we were doing refereeing match preparation years before it became common in international rugby.

Every other game, an assessor from the Norfolk Referees Society would turn up to watch me and write a report on my performance. Half the time, I'd be missing an eyebrow or half of my hair would be dyed blond, or white with black spots, like a dalmatian.

'You're the referee?'

'Yes, I do apologise . . .'

There was also the time I streaked at a game of crown green bowls, not knowing that one of the bowlers was chairman of the Norfolk RFU. A couple of weeks later, he came up to me at a refereeing event and said, 'I recognise you, don't I?' I told him I didn't think so, and he replied, 'Yes, you do. I've seen your arse . . .'

But I must have done all right, because by the end of my third year, when I was twenty-one, I'd reached Level 5. And the Rugby Football Union invited me to interview for the National Panel, which is the top fifty referees in England.

GIVING UP THE GAME

If I took up their offer, I'd probably be the youngest referee ever selected. The snag being, the RFU required its referees to stop playing, to reduce the chances of injury, and I thought it was way too early to hang my boots up. As far as I was concerned, they still had a lot of dancing to do.

I'd had a few injuries in my teens, but now I felt I'd finally grown into my legs and was beginning to hit my stride. I also thought my refereeing had made me more tactically astute, and therefore a key strategic weapon for my team. So I informed the RFU that I'd need some time to think about it.

While I was weighing up my future, I looked back on some of my career highlights. There were UEA's games against Her Majesty's Prison Wayland, where they locked us in before kick-off, the referee was a screw, and we always let them win because we were terrified of what they would do to us if we didn't. I'll never forget the time one of our players scored a try, forgot where he was and started screaming in an opponent's face. He was lucky not to get twatted.

Then there was our glorious procession to the Norfolk Plate final. No one wanted a university team to win the Norfolk Plate because, understandably, they hated students (and we didn't have a clubhouse). In an attempt to nobble us, the organisers would schedule games during our holidays, but we were always able to cobble together fifteen players, whether it was Christmas or Easter.

Our opponents in the final were Crusaders, a notoriously niggly team from the village of Little Melton, population 897 (presumably 882 on the day of the final, or 877 if you include replacements). Having annoyed some of my teammates by playing too many Carpenters songs on the way there (most of them took their rugby more seriously than me), our bus pulled into Crusaders' car park rocking to 'Eye of the Tiger', meaning we were all quite fired up.

I say my game had improved, but I was still a non-tackling back row. So my main role in the team was to cheat. We had a move that involved me holding on to the back of the opposition flanker's shirt, which allowed us to slip down the blindside. But the first time I tried it against Crusaders, the bloke just smashed me in the face. I turned to the touch judge, who I knew, and screeched, 'He can't do that!' He replied, 'You can't be holding on to him either!'

Besides the splattered nose, it was a magnificent game, from which we emerged victorious. The plate we won made it back to Norwich, where our coach, who was pretty hacked off with how we'd been treated that season, frisbeed it across the university square. We spent the rest of the evening smashing it over each other's heads so that it ended up resembling a giant poppadom. The coach had to buy a replacement, and I've still got the original in my study.

One night after training, I sat my teammates down, asked for silence and, with some trepidation, explained my dilemma. 'I'm in two minds,' I told them. 'I enjoy refereeing, but I don't want to let you guys down.'

I hadn't expected them to sob, but I had hoped they would spend some time discussing the ramifications for the team. Instead, there was a short pause, followed by audible sighs of relief, followed by sniggers, followed by uproarious laughter. My playing career had come to an end, and nobody gave a shit.

Only after appointing me to the National Panel did the RFU realise I still hadn't done any refereeing courses. The most I'd done was push tiny players around a Subbuteo table at Gloucester and District Referees Society meetings.

I know it sounds mad, becoming an established referee without any qualifications, but you learn far more from refereeing actual games. That's why my advice to young referees is always, 'Referee as much as you can, because you'll learn from your mistakes.'

After a while, things you once had to think about become instinctive, especially positioning. For example, after being run over a few times at lineouts, I worked out which channels not to stand in. It's about learning to *feel* the game, rather than constantly having to rifle through a rule book in your head.

The next refereeing exam was on a Tuesday evening in London, which was no good to me, so Dave Broadwell, who was an RFU rugby manager, and Paul Storey, an RFU coach, drove up to Norwich and I did the exam in my university digs.

The digs were a disgusting eight-bedroom house with mould growing all over the walls and ceilings. In some lesser-used rooms, toadstools had sprouted. I did the exam on a filthy table in my bedroom, which didn't have toadstools but was probably home to dozens of unidentified bacteria.

Dave and Paul were staying in Norwich, so I dragged them along to a student night at Liquid. I say 'dragged', but they were mad for it, despite having a combined age of about a hundred.

I spent most of my time at UEA wishing I'd done another subject. I was only interested in criminal law, stuff like how to prosecute someone for GBH, so writing an essay about some obscure constitutional case from 1702, or a woman who sued a drinks manufacturer after finding a snail at the bottom of her bottle in the 1920s, didn't hold much interest for me.

But because most of my mates were doing four-year courses or tagging on a Master's degree, and I didn't want to leave without them – the fear of missing out on all that idiocy would have been too much to bear – I applied for and got the student union communications officer role, largely thanks to my rugby mates, who weighed in with some flagrant voter intimidation.

I had the most wonderful few years at UEA and, despite hating my course, I emerged a Bachelor of Law. I was also an RFU National Panel referee and the proud member of the best group of mates a bloke could ask for.

Fast forward nearly twenty years, and I'm on stage at UEA's Haydn Morris Hall, dressed in a traditional robe and big, floppy hat, accepting an honorary doctorate. But I'm somewhat distracted by my phone, which won't stop buzzing in my pocket. When I get the chance, I nip to the toilet to find out who's been congratulating me. The first text I open reads: 'I didn't know you could get a doctorate for being a shit ref.' The rest are variations on that theme.

But who wants mates who are nice to you all the time? Not me. And we're all really close to this day. We've watched sport together all over the world, from the Tour de France when it went to Denmark to hurling in Munster, and that camaraderie was sparked by our shared love of rugby. A few of the lads are still active, including one who plays second row for Winchester, at the age of forty-two. In case you were wondering, Candle has a new car and he looks after it very well.

3

Imposter Syndrome

Towards the end of a law degree, you have to decide whether you want to be a barrister or a solicitor. It was an easy choice for me, because of all that *Kavanagh QC*.

To become a barrister, you have to do what was then called a barrister vocation course, which is a year learning advocacy, debating, drafting and the rest. The problem was, it was bloody expensive – about ten grand, which didn't include accommodation. I had no financial support from my parents or savings (and they wonder why there are so few barristers from working-class backgrounds), so was flailing a bit until someone told me the Inns of Court, which are the four professional associations of barristers, offered scholarships.

I applied for a scholarship to one of the four, Lincoln's Inn in London, and, to my surprise, they invited me down for an interview. Surprise turned to shock a few weeks later when I received a letter explaining that not only were they going to pay for my scholarship, but they were also going to pay for my accommodation, a flat right at the heart of the Inn.

Besides the interview, I'd only been to London once before, when I saw *Starlight Express* as a thirteen-year-old schoolboy. So I'll never forget being dropped off by my then girlfriend one Sunday evening. She gave me a kiss on the cheek, wished me luck, got back into her clapped-out Renault and headed home. And I was suddenly alone, feeling a lot like Dick Whittington.

Goodness me, it was all a bit bewildering for a boy from the Forest of Dean. Lincoln's Inn is in the City, which virtually shuts down on weekends. But I managed to find a newsagent that sold A–Z street maps and headed to the bright lights and seedy streets of Soho. When I got there, my first thought was, *Wow, this place looks brilliant. I think I could have a lot of fun here* . . .

For the next twelve months, I learned everything there was to learn about the trade from the Inn's senior barristers. As part of the professional qualification, you have to dine in your chosen Inn twelve times during the year, and it was over food and drink that a lot of my learning was done.

Despite the scholarship and free flat, I struggled financially. Luckily, I've always had people looking out for me. A fellow ref worked in a nearby bank, and he arranged for me to use their gym for free. Meanwhile, the RFU gave me some holiday work, filing and what not, which kept my head above water.

About a thousand people each year do the barrister vocation course, but only about a hundred of them will get pupillage, which is basically a training contract. For the first six months, you shadow a barrister, learning from and working for them. Then you take your first baby steps as a barrister, usually in magistrates' court, under the watchful eye of a senior colleague.

I applied for about fifty pupillages and was rejected from most within a few weeks. I got one interview, but that didn't go anywhere, which meant there was only one chambers left.

I thought the dream was over, until I was on the train home from a game in Cambridge one Wednesday night and my mobile beeped. When I pressed the button, it said I had thirty-four voicemails. For some reason, I hadn't been receiving them for a week. Most of them were from Mum, asking why I hadn't rung home for ages. But there was also a message from the clerk at 3 Temple Gardens, asking if I'd like to come in for an interview with the pupillage committee, some time between Tuesday and Thursday the following week. Alas, it already was the following week.

On Thursday morning, I got up early, rang the clerk and asked if they could possibly fit me in that evening. The answer was a flat no, and that I'd have to apply next year. I explained the situation, and kept apologising profusely, but the clerk, a formidable woman called Sue, was not for turning. I refused to give up, however, and eventually Sue said she'd speak to the pupillage committee. And at about 5.30, she phoned to say they'd fit me in at 7.15

– before making it quite clear that they were doing me a favour.

I wasn't expecting the interview to lead to anything – I kept thinking that maybe I hadn't gone to the 'right' school and was full of regret for not trying harder at university. Besides, they'd have thought I was a shambles whatever school I'd gone to or degree I'd got.

But the first thing they did when I walked into the committee room was offer me a glass of wine. And it looked like they'd had a few already. Between the three of them, they didn't mention law once during the interview, which wasn't really an interview at all. All they wanted to know was whether I could get them free rugby tickets.

Two days later, Sue called to let me know that they wanted me to join 3 Temple Gardens as a pupil. Not getting those messages did me a big favour, because it meant I'd ambushed the committee after a hard day's work, when they were more interested in rugby and wine than the law.

My pupil master for the first six months – think Yoda and Luke Skywalker – was Wayne Cleaver, which was weird, seeing as there were only three barristers called Wayne in the whole of England, including me.

Most pupils and masters would go their separate ways after court, but I followed my fellow Wayne everywhere. We'd often have dinner together, and sometimes even end up in Soho, drinking until midnight.

My pupil master for the second six months, when I was doing cases myself, was Brian Stork. His main job was to make sure I didn't make any major screw-ups, and thankfully I didn't. Brian and I became close as well, and not just because he was a massive rugby fan and still after those tickets.

When the twelve months were up, I applied for tenancy. That involved some advocacy, as witnessed by members of the chambers, followed by an interview, which consisted of lots of questions as to why I wanted to be a barrister, specifically at 3 Temple Gardens.

Tradition dictates that tenancy applications take place on Thursdays, and that the committee deliberates before giving you their decision later that night. When I headed to the pub to meet my university mates, I wasn't at all optimistic because about one in five pupils fails to get tenancy, and almost no one who gets one went to the University of East Anglia.

I was in a godforsaken pub called Strawberry Moons in Soho when the call came from John Coffey QC, the head of chambers. 'Hello, Wayne,' he said, 'we'd be delighted if you'd join us.' Cue carnage, fuelled by cider, sambuca and Asti Spumante, rather than champagne. But the size and length of those celebrations were justified, because I'd just been given a dream job for life.

It's tradition that the morning after the night before, the new kid has to work. So after three hours' sleep, I dragged myself out of bed and headed to Blackfriars Crown Court. Thankfully, my duties weren't onerous – I certainly didn't get anyone out of jail – and I was back in chambers by midday.

I felt like a bit of a fraud strolling around in my horsehair wig and gown, which my great-grandma (who was affectionately known as Nanny Moaner, because she moaned a lot) had saved up to buy me from Ede & Ravenscroft, the tailors who have been operating on Chancery Lane for almost 350 years. (Nanny Moaner must have been saving up for a long time, because that wig and gown cost about £700, at a time when I was earning £46.50 a day.) I'd catch a glimpse of myself in the mirror and think, *Blimey, am I really a barrister?*

The first person I bumped into back at chambers was Wayne Cleaver, with whom I repaired to the Middle Temple Bar. That was a historic day for 3 Temple Gardens, because they took on three of us, which they'd never done before. And when three new tenants and their masters/mistresses celebrate together, things can get messy.

This time, there was champagne instead of Asti. A lot of it. Normally, this wouldn't have been a problem. But it was in this case, because I was refereeing my first Premiership game the following day: Bath v. Rotherham at the famous Rec. And I had no idea if I was ready for it or not.

When I was coming through the ranks, and regularly refereeing at Levels 2 and 3, Andy Melrose, an RFU referee coach, invited me to a game between Wasps and Gloucester at Loftus Road (QPR's ground) to get a better idea of what it took to officiate in the Premiership.

A Welshman called Nigel Williams was in charge, and I thought, *There's no way I'm ever going to be able to do what he's doing.* So many things were happening at once, and they were all happening so fast, so I couldn't understand why Nigel was making some of his decisions.

I was still reffing games like Chingford v. Campion Old Boys in the Essex Cup final, which were slightly more sedate affairs (although I did have to send off a Campion player in that one). And I'd sometimes walk off the pitch after an average performance and wonder if I'd ever be good enough to make the step up.

One such game was Moseley v. Worcester, in National Division One. Moseley had a hard, nuggety hooker called Richard Protherough who had a reputation for fighting. Early in proceedings, he landed a couple on one of his opponents, Tony Windo, and I thought, *I'll lay a marker down here.* I pulled a card from my left pocket and showed it to Protherough, with a flourish, and he gave me a disbelieving look before trudging off.

About fifteen minutes later, I said to one of the Moseley players, 'Where's Protherough gone? He should be back on by now.' And the bloke replied, 'You sent him off, you twat.' That's when I realised I'd put my cards in the wrong pockets – it was always yellow left, red right – and I just had to style things out. Rather than admitting my mistake and apologising, I wrote my report as it happened and Protherough got a three-week ban.

I hadn't even considered how I was going to get from London to Bath. But at some point during the evening's festivities, I had a moment of clarity, phoned my best mate Ox (one of the UEA contingent) and told him I was in a bit of a pickle. Ox told me to make my way to Twickenham, where he'd pick me up and drive me down.

My mate stayed overnight at his girlfriend's while I slept it off at the Hilton. When I awoke in the morning, I felt very average. But kick-off wasn't until 3 p.m., and how hard could Bath versus struggling Rotherham be?

Bath were top of the table, while Rotherham were bottom after four straight defeats. That's why I was given the game, because everyone expected Bath to romp it (plus, all our international referees were at the 2003 World Cup in Australia).

My hangover actually did me a favour because it knocked the edge off my nerves. I was more worried about making it through the game without being sick than getting any big decisions wrong. Still, there were some formidable names on the team sheet, particularly in the front row, with Bath's England props David Flatman and Duncan Bell up against Rotherham tight-head Simon Bunting, who had a reputation as a complete lunatic.

God knows what Simon thought when he first laid eyes on me, this gangly twenty-four-year-old who would have been at least five years younger than him. I imagine it was something along the lines of, *Maybe with this callow youth as the referee, I can take a few more liberties than normal . . .*

Things were going smoothly until a punch-up midway through the first half. I thought, *This is my chance to show I'm not to be trifled with*, blew my whistle a few times and jumped in to break things up. As if by magic, the players suddenly stopped throwing punches and parted, just as a huge cheer went up from the crowd. I thought, *That was easy, and it's nice that the fans appreciated my efforts.* But when I looked over my shoulder, I saw a streaker running around in an elephant posing pouch and waving the trunk around.

Bath were well ahead after sixty minutes, so I was confident I wouldn't have to make any match-deciding decisions. But just as a lineout was about to be taken, Andy Melrose, one of my touch judges, started shouting at me down his flag to stop the game (in those days, a touch judge's flag doubled as a walkie-talkie).

At first, I thought it must have been another punch-up, but that didn't make sense because I could see all the players. Then I thought that maybe the streaker had got loose again. It was only when I saw an ambulance driving straight down the middle of the pitch that I realised what had happened. A fan had collapsed in the stand, and that was the quickest way to reach him.

So that was my first experience of top-class rugby: a punch-up, a streaker and a collapsed fan, with a bit of rugby in between. For the record, Bath won 47–3, I didn't have to make any big decisions, and me and four of my mates, who'd come to support me, drank champagne all the way back to London, me wedged in the middle of the back seat of a three-door VW Polo.

The champagne was justified because I'd got tenancy and refereed my first Premiership game in the space of two days. But I still felt like I was stumbling into things and just about getting away with it. I suppose you'd call that imposter syndrome.

— ★ —

A few months into my first Premiership season, I was handed my first real test, London Irish v. Sale at the Madejski Stadium in Reading.

In their previous game, only a month earlier, a Sale player had punched Irish number eight Chris Sheasby and he'd suffered a fractured eye socket (that makes me feel old, because Sheasby made his debut for Wasps in the 1980s), so this one was expected to be a tight, fiery encounter. And that's exactly how it panned out.

I could feel the aggro from the outset, and I thought the best way to deal with it was to give as many penalties as possible from the start, in the hope that it would discourage the players from going overboard. It didn't work. It was a bitter game, played in torrential rain, and I had to yellow card both Sale props before the break.

Irish ended up winning 9–3, no tries were scored and Sale's Jason Robinson, who'd just won the World Cup with England, got the biggest cheer of the afternoon and he didn't even play. But there was so much niggle going on, and it was all happening quicker than I was used to. It was the first time since my playing career that I'd felt that out of my depth on a rugby field.

But refereeing is like anything else in that the more you do it, the clearer things become. Batting in cricket is a good analogy: the first time a ball comes at you at 90 mph, you're not going to see it very well, if at all. And you're probably going to be nervous. But the more you face bowling of that speed, the quicker you'll be able to react and the less nervous you'll be. Similarly, the more I refereed in the Premiership,

44

the more attuned my eyes became, and the more confident I was of making the right decisions. Everything seemed slower than it used to, and I seemed to have more time to get into the right positions.

Still, I didn't do much in the way of preparation in the early days. The RFU's refereeing coach would have a chat with me before a game, tell me which players might give me a bit of grief, and also make sure I had two experienced touch judges, who'd give me a pep talk before kick-off. But I wouldn't speak to the coaches or even know all the players on the team sheet, let alone the ins and outs of Simon Bunting's scrummaging technique.

One player I didn't need to do much homework on was Martin Johnson, England's World Cup-winning captain, who had been terrifying referees for well over a decade before I came on the scene.

I refereed Johnno twice in two weeks in his final season, the first time when Leicester played Leeds Tykes at Welford Road. As with most of my early games, it was expected to be a one-sided affair, but Welford Road was always intimidating in those days. Having only refereed five or six games the previous season (after the international refs returned from World Cup duty, I was surplus to requirements most weekends), it was quite a punchy appointment for a rookie like me.

Players and officials emerged from the changing room under the Crumbie Stand, as it was still called back then, and entered the field of play through a tunnel of fans, some of them within touching distance. And once the game started,

I was meant to be in charge of not only Johnno, but also a host of other World Cup winners. When you've got 25,000 Leicester fans screaming at you, plus the likes of Johnno, Neil Back and Will Greenwood chirping in your ear, it's very challenging for a referee to keep a clear mind.

I'm six foot three, which comes in handy as a rugby referee, because I'm not usually dwarfed while I'm telling players off. But the really big blokes can intimidate a referee just by standing close to them – they don't need histrionics, like footballers, because their presence is enough. So it was with Johnno, who made me look like a little boy at the coin toss – and probably thought I was.

Luckily, Leicester gave Leeds a bit of a tonking that day, and Johnno got one of the tries, so I wasn't mentioned in the reports, which is always a good thing. But the second and final time I refereed Johnno, when Leicester played London Irish in Reading the following week, was a different case entirely.

Thirty seconds into the game, Johnno set up Martin Corry for a try. But not long after that, Johnno smashed into Irish full-back Delon Armitage about half an hour late (he probably called it a professional foul, but most people called it a cheap shot), I blew my whistle and a horrible thought occurred to me: *I'm gonna have to sinbin him. Oh, bugger.*

People forget that referees are fans. Like everyone else in the country, I was cheering for England in the World Cup final (I refereed in Worcester that day and almost missed kick-off because the game went to extra time and I had to drive up from Bream) and had also watched Johnno captain the Lions to victory in South Africa in 1997, so he was a massive hero of mine.

I fumbled in my pocket, pulled out my yellow card and said, 'I'm sorry, sir.' I don't think I even brandished it. Johnno clambered to his feet, raised himself to his full height, glared at me under those beetling brows and said, 'That's the only fucking decision you've got right so far . . .' If I'd seen the two punches he landed on Irish lock Bob Casey just before half-time, I'd have had to send him off.

There's a horrible clip of me telling off Martin Corry and Bath's Steve Borthwick, neither as big nor as intimidating as Johnno, but still serious units. They were also future England captains, and I was addressing them like a headmaster would two naughty boys in his office: 'This is outrageous behaviour, you're supposed to set an example, you both need to calm down . . .'

That's how I thought I needed to manage players back then, to 'command' respect, but when I see that clip now, I wince and squirm, because I'm screaming and shouting and it's me who needs to calm down.

I also wonder why they listened to me and what they were thinking. *Who the hell does this pipsqueak think he is? Didn't this game deserve someone more important?* Then I think of the big, tough blokes I sent off when I was still only fifteen or sixteen, or the middle-aged skippers who called me sir. How did I get away with it for so long? How was it even allowed?

People assume I must have been one of those precocious, annoyingly confident kids. In truth, I was blissfully unaware. Eddie Jones once said to me, 'Referees are the same as players – they're at their best at the start and end of their careers, because that's when they don't think or worry as much.' I agree with that assessment, because I spent a lot of my early career not really knowing what I was doing, which meant I wasn't too whistle-happy.

Also, whatever the likes of Corry and Borthwick were thinking, they didn't want to be seen on TV arguing with a referee who still looked like a teenager, just like the blokes I refereed back in the Forest of Dean didn't want to be seen arguing with me when I *was* a teenager. Being a bit of a freak was still working for me.

4

Boys on Tour

My colleagues at 3 Temple Gardens were very understanding of my second job, not least when I asked if I could continue officiating on the sevens circuit.

Galivanting around the world for weeks at a time limited my chances as a barrister because it meant I couldn't represent anyone in a long trial, as you can't just put a case on hold while you hop on a plane to Hong Kong or Dubai. But the sevens circuit is the most enjoyment a rugby referee can have, especially if he's in his mid-twenties.

I did my first sevens games in 2002, a year before I made my Premiership debut. I started out as an in-goal referee, which is the person who tracks up and down to see if the ball is grounded. My first tournament was at Twickenham, and I got really stuck into the free booze the night before.

The older officials had told me we were due to meet at 9.30 a.m., but I got a call from the referees' boss at 7.40 a.m., telling me everyone had been waiting for me in reception since 7.30. I apologised profusely, brushed my teeth, grabbed my bag and legged it downstairs, as fast as my very rubbery legs would carry me. The referees' boss was fuming, while my fellow officials were laughing their heads off.

I'd only had about three hours' sleep, but still managed to make it through the first few hours without any issues. But later, after God knows how many games, I wandered up to a post, put my head against the padding and promptly fell asleep. It was only two or three seconds – one of those micro-sleeps you hear about – and it was a one-sided game, with most of the attacking happening at the other end. But when you're falling asleep in the middle of a game at Twickenham, you should probably rein things in a bit.

As with players – think Lawrence Dallaglio, Josh Lewsey and Danny Care, who all played sevens for their clubs and England – the shrunken version of the game used to be a training ground for referees, and it taught me three big lessons: how to officiate in packed, rowdy stadiums (you'd get 45,000 in Hong Kong), how to be a harmonious member of a team of officials (if you can get through two weeks without pissing off any of your colleagues, you've done okay), and the importance of getting to know players, who you might end up refereeing in fifteens.

But because sevens is a simpler game usually played in a less pressured environment, us referees had an awful lot of fun away from the field. One week we'd be in

Dubai, the next in George, South Africa, then Brisbane, then Wellington, then Los Angeles, then Hong Kong, then Cardiff, then Twickenham. We'd do a bit of training, but most of the time it was sightseeing and drinking. I'd even catch up on legal stuff, if the hangover wasn't too bad.

Our refereeing gang, which totalled six or seven blokes, included Nigel Owens and Craig Joubert, and the three of us quickly became close. When we were in George, I stayed with Craig's family and hung out with his mates. I always used to tell Craig that he seemed more English than South African, in that he had a sense of humour. Also like me, Craig was in his twenties, so up for lots of fun. As were most of the players.

After the George tournament, we arrived back at our hotel to find England's Kai Horstmann asleep on a bench outside. We picked him up and dragged him to his room, which was no mean feat given that he was six foot three and sixteen stone. Kai went on to be a stalwart for Worcester Warriors and Exeter, and he never forgot that time I saved him from a potentially sticky situation.

I also vaguely remember a big party with all the players after the Wellington sevens, which was always a big tournament. The next morning, we staggered on to a plane, got pissed again, landed in LA on Super Bowl Sunday, and went straight back out. Because of the time difference, we technically got pissed three times in one day. We then had two days off, so the boys and I drove the referees' minibus to Las Vegas. While we were there, our manager called to suggest a meeting, and one of us had to tell him we were 270 miles away from LA, losing all our money in a casino.

Despite his public persona, Nige is quite reserved. When he came to my wedding, the other guests expected him to be leading the charge, necking drinks and dancing on tables, but he's not like that – unless he's got an audience and a microphone in his hand, when you can't stop him singing.

Nige sang 'How Great Thou Art' at my wedding, and everywhere we went on the sevens circuit, we'd end up in the corner of some bar, belting out songs – Nige rather well, Craig less so, me appallingly, like Vic Reeves's club singer.

On occasion, I'd don my barrister's wig and conduct a kangaroo court, which would basically be an excuse to make Nige and Craig neck daft drinks. The next time I put the wig on for an actual trial, I'd notice a footprint on it or that some of the curls had unravelled.

Nowadays, referees aren't allowed to drink between tournaments, and there aren't many parties anyway. The career-wrecking combination of camera phones and social media has pretty much snuffed out some of the stuff we got up to on the sevens circuit back then, while it's no longer seen as a natural progression to the fifteen-a-side game, either for players or officials. That's a shame because, partying aside, I learned an awful lot from the sevens circuit, particularly from Nige and Craig, who went on to be two of the finest refs ever.

Another progression for up-and-coming referees was the Under-19s World Cup, or a version of it run by Rugby

Europe (FIRA). I was invited to officiate at the 2003 tournament in Paris, which was actually in Marcoussis, a godforsaken suburb about twenty miles south of the city.

Marcoussis is a one-horse town with a railway station that stops running at about 7 p.m. I think it has a bistro, and it may or may not have a coffee shop. The French senior team train there, and apparently the players call it 'Marcoutraz', because it's almost impossible to escape from.

The tournament had lots of rest days, so I spent a lot of time in the Pigalle area of Paris, which is famous for the Moulin Rouge and sex shops. To be fair, I didn't have a choice in the matter. I was very much led by a couple of Celtic referees who had been around the block a few times, seemed to know exactly what was what and enjoyed stitching up naive twenty-three-year-olds.

I also spent a lot of time in a bar owned by an old university mate, Danny Williams, and because of the train situation in Marcoutraz, most of my per diems – the daily allowance – went on taxis, usually hailed at 3 a.m. or later. Sadly, our manager was a big fan of 6 a.m. pool recovery sessions, which were compulsory whether you'd been involved in a game the day before or not. Some mornings, I'd creep back into my hotel room, change into my swimming shorts and head straight to the pool.

My first taste of senior international rugby was in November 2002, when I was an assistant ref for a World Cup qualifier between Russia and Spain.

The game should have taken place a couple of weeks earlier in Krasnoyarsk, Siberia, but was called off because of snow, funnily enough. That evening, the referee slipped on ice and busted his leg, so Jonathan Kaplan was flown over from South Africa for the rescheduled fixture in Krasnodar, which is down on the Black Sea, while I was called up at the last minute to run touch.

The night before the game, the other officials and I were taken out by representatives of the Russian rugby federation. In Russia, it's tradition to toast in twos, because toasting in odd numbers is bad luck. And remember, they toast pretty much everything. There were shots of vodka before the meal, shots of vodka between courses, and even more shots of vodka afterwards. An older me would have stopped toasting at some point, to hell with local tradition, but the younger me was only too happy to neck every shot on offer.

We ended up in a hotel bar that was like something from a James Bond film. As the night wore on, the lighting became dimmer and the women more numerous. And I also noticed that they were wearing fewer and fewer clothes.

At some point, one of the Russian officials made me an offer they presumably thought I couldn't refuse: 'If you can help us win tomorrow's game, you can have the pick of these ladies.' I thought, *Prostitution isn't really my thing. But is this just what happens before internationals?* I politely declined, made my excuses and scurried back to our hotel.

The game was played in an athletics stadium that only had two changing rooms, so the officials had to get ready in a hotel about 400 metres away. We ran to the stadium in full kit, including studs, led by two armed guards. We had to go straight across the market square, and because Russians aren't really into rugby, the locals had no idea who or what the hell we were.

Spain won on the day, but Russia won on aggregate. Only in the bar afterwards, when one of the Russian props asked if we could swap shirts, did I think that something might be amiss. One Russian prop, whose nickname was Tank, sounded suspiciously South African. And because South Africans have a distinct accent, particularly in a Russian bar, I soon discovered there were a couple more of them in attendance.

The following day, an International Rugby Board (IRB) liaison officer asked to see the players' passports, and the team manager tried to pull the old Obi-Wan Kenobi Jedi mind trick: 'You don't need to see our identification.' It didn't work. Russia were disqualified for fielding three ineligible players.

In April 2005, at the age of twenty-five, I became the RFU's youngest ever full-time elite referee. There were only six of us in England, including Chris 'Whitey' White, a fellow Gloucestershire lad who'd done two World Cups, and Tony 'Spreaders' Spreadbury, who refereed his first Test in 1990. And the following year, I was invited to referee at the inaugural Pacific 5 Nations (later the Pacific Nations Cup).

My first game was the Junior All Blacks versus Tonga in New Plymouth, which isn't exactly a rugby hotbed. A few thousand people turned up to watch, the Junior All Blacks won comfortably, and the game passed without incident. But the following week, I refereed my first international, Fiji versus Samoa, which was a far juicier proposition.

I flew to Fiji with Kiwi ref Jonathon White, who was (and still is) a top cardiologist. We stayed near Nadi, which is on the opposite coast to Suva, and spent a week exploring. The locals were so welcoming and so keen to show off their country. And everywhere we went, we'd see villagers, young and old, playing touch rugby in jungle clearings. There was so much talent on display, and some of those youngsters probably went on to represent their country.

On the eve of the game, we drove all the way to Suva (the potholes were more like craters, but there were no internal flights), and when we arrived at the ground I was surprised to find it had no stands. Still, something like 8,000 fans gathered on the grass banks, while the VIPs were seated under a little green awning. Guest of honour was Commodore Frank Bainimarama, head of the Fijian Armed Forces, and my then girlfriend was seated next to him.

When I went to say hello to her before kick-off, she was primly drinking tea out of a delicate bone-china cup, as was Frank. She said to me, 'Oh, this is Commodore Frank,' as if she was introducing me to some bloke she'd got chatting to on the bus. Commodore Frank told me he was going to look after my girlfriend while I was running around and wished me luck for the game ahead.

As is customary in games between Fiji and Samoa, some of the hits were X-rated. And the noise from the crowd whenever a defender raced out of the line and chopped down some poor soul who had left his ribs exposed was ear-splitting.

After twenty-seven minutes, Fijian wing Mosese Luveitasau picked up a Samoan player and dropped him on his head, so I had to show him a red card. Luckily for me, Fiji somehow managed to hang on for a narrow win (Commodore Frank might have shown me his dark side had they not), and I got straight on the kava, not the fizzy stuff they drink in Spain, but the national tipple of Fiji.

My drinking partner was Fiji lock and skipper Simon Raiwalui – and going kava for kava with Simon is as ill-advised as drinking pints of lager with Jason Leonard. Kava doesn't exactly get you drunk, but it numbs everything and is supposed to make you euphoric. I just felt like I was going to die.

Commodore Frank, I was told, was a wonderful matchday host, so I was quite surprised when I learned that he'd taken control of the country by coup d'état a few months later. I said to my girlfriend, 'What the hell did you say to him while you were watching the game? Did you put any daft ideas in his head?' Whatever they spoke about that day, he stayed in charge for sixteen years.

I've done so many games like that, in weird and wonderful places. That's when you really get to know the players and coaches, although the hospitality sometimes goes out of the window if the home team doesn't get the win.

Another of my early games was a World Cup qualifier between Morocco and Portugal in Casablanca. We were greeted at the airport by the president of the Moroccan rugby federation, who I think was also the chairman, treasurer, sponge man and, apparently, driver.

He whisked us straight to his house, where we were greeted by other members of the Moroccan rugby federation, who all seemed to have the same surname as him. Over the next couple of days, we were wined and dined like we'd never been wined and dined before. I must have put on half a stone. And when we weren't wining and dining, we were in a steam bath or getting a full body scrub from the president/chairman/treasurer/sponge man/driver's cousin.

But after the game, which Portugal won 10–5, we waited ages for the promised lift to the airport, until it dawned on us that it had been cancelled without our knowledge. At that point, I made a mental note: *If you're ever back in Casablanca, give the full body scrub a miss. You might end up getting garrotted* . . .

It was all a far cry from being an international football referee. Those guys get ferried everywhere in blacked-out limousines, and if anyone found out they were being entertained by members of the local football federation, they would never work as a referee again.

In 2008, I was Nige's assistant for a game between France and the Pacific Islanders, which took place in Montbéliard, a small town on the Swiss border (which would be roughly equivalent to England playing an international in Barnstaple).

The Pacific Islanders are a combination of Fiji, Samoa and Tonga, so they're normally pretty good – and often very physical. The Islanders were leading 6–3 after eighteen minutes, when France scrum-half Jean-Baptiste Élissalde kicked to touch. When someone kicks to touch, the referee will usually follow the ball, while the touch judge will keep his eyes on the kicker to check whether anyone hits him late. But I was already running upfield with my flag raised when I heard a chorus of jeers from the crowd. And when I looked over my shoulder, I saw Élissalde laid out on his back, completely out of the game.

While the medics were trying to bring Élissalde back to life, Nige and I assessed the situation. We both knew some seriously foul play had occurred, but neither of us had seen anything, and this was before television match officials. Nige decided there was nothing we could do, when suddenly a replay flashed up on the big screen: the Islanders' Fijian winger Napoloni Nalaga, who played for Clermont in the French Top 14, had hit Élissalde about two seconds late and almost removed his head from his shoulders.

My first reaction was, *I've missed this terrible high tackle because I followed the ball, which I've been taught never to do.* Then I thought, *We're not allowed to send people off using screens – what the hell happens now?*

Nige and I had a little chat before I concluded I'd seen the incident in real time. Off went Nalaga, followed by Élissalde on a stretcher, and in Nige's match report, he said something along the lines of, 'After seeing the incident, we had no hesitation in awarding a red card.'

After the game, which France won 42–17, Nige and I were invited to a party at the Moulin Rouge – not the famous cabaret in Paris, but the region's premier discotheque.

We hitched a lift with the Islanders, and when we got on the bus, Nige was directed to an empty seat next to a beaming Napolioni Nalaga, the bloke he'd just sent off. Everyone found that hilarious, and Nige was soon belting out hymns and arias in that beautiful Welsh baritone of his.

If it's a bad idea to drink kava with Fijians in Fiji, it's an even worse idea to drink French firewater with a mix of Fijians, Samoans and Tongans. At some point, I decided to get a cab back to the hotel with another touch judge, but Nige was enjoying himself far too much and stuck around for more.

Nige didn't speak a word of French, and we were in a part of France where not many people spoke English (or indeed Welsh). He finally managed to persuade another reveller to give him a lift home (drink driving was still de rigueur in Montbéliard), but when the bloke dropped him off, he suddenly demanded money.

Nige thought, *I'm not giving him any money, he never told me he was a taxi,* but when he tried to walk off without paying, the bloke followed him into the hotel. The hotel had a big spiral staircase and, as Nige was trying to get up it, this bloke was hanging on to his leg. Nige eventually managed to kick the bloke off, but no sooner had he barricaded himself in his room than this fake taxi driver was banging on his door while screaming and shouting in French.

When Nige told me this story the following morning, my first question was, 'At what point did you think it was a good idea to get a lift home from some random Frenchman?' But looking back, it was just another of those strange situations us rugby referees find ourselves in from time to time.

5

Politics

Rugby is more about politics than most people will ever know. And I learned quite early in my refereeing career that relationships are often more important than your ability to do the job.

In 2005, I went to the Under-21s World Cup in Mendoza, Argentina, where I refereed the opening game between Wales and New Zealand. New Zealand won convincingly, but I stayed out of the way and there were no mentions of me in the media. All in all, I thought I'd performed pretty well.

We'd been asked to keep a close eye on a particular aspect of offside, namely attackers standing in front of the ball at the ruck. I didn't think the odd player standing in front of the ball made much difference, and I was against penalising the attacking side, because it interfered with the flow of the game.

But the referee manager made it clear how important this new directive was, and I'd been advised just to go along with whatever I was told at tournaments ('Listen, nod, wear your shirt and tie whenever you're told to', the sort of stuff that makes you feel a bit sick when you're listening to it), so I penalised most of the offsides in question, while probably missing a couple.

After the first round of games, we had a review with the referee manager, a guy called Steve Griffiths. Steve showed some examples of us failing to implement this new offside directive, before asking if everyone was okay with it. We all nodded, but Steve wanted to probe a bit deeper.

'Right then, Barnesy,' he said, 'what do you really think?'

'I've obviously missed one or two,' I replied, 'but I appreciate the feedback and I'll keep doing my best to catch them.'

'I know you will, Barnesy. But what do you *really* think?'

Maybe I should have bitten my tongue, but instead I said, 'Well, since you've asked me twice now, I don't believe in it. They're not having any effect on play, and we're penalising the attacking team, when we're meant to be encouraging attacking rugby. But don't worry, I'll continue to do what I'm told.'

Steve came back with, 'So what other laws don't you want to referee?'

'Well,' I said, 'you can start with crooked feeds at the scrum,' before reeling off three or four more laws that were regularly ignored.

I knew none of the other referees were okay with this new directive, because they were all saying the same as me behind the scenes. But the only one who backed me up was Marius Jonker, who has always been a good friend.

For the rest of the tournament, I refereed games between lower-ranked teams, including the eleventh/twelfth-placed play-off (there were only twelve teams there). And because none of those games mattered in the grand scheme of things, I spent a lot of time with the local refs, who treated me as if I was some sort of celebrity after speaking my mind.

For a while after that tournament, I thought my way to becoming an international referee would be hampered. As it was, Steve was soon replaced by a Kiwi called Paddy O'Brien, who rang me and said, 'I heard you upset Griff, which made me laugh. So we're going to give you a chance.' And the following summer, I was in Suva, refereeing my first international between Fiji and Samoa.

Marius and I were the only two guys from that Under-21s World Cup who went on to referee internationals, so maybe there is something to be said for displaying your personality and speaking your mind. That's why I say to younger refs now, even in front of management, 'The only thing that will make you a better referee is not listening to the constant advice you get. There's a reason you're an international referee, and that's because you've got something about you, not because of any directives you've had from above.'

A good example of the benefits of digging your heels in is when the television match official (TMO) protocol changed, and it started to be used for foul play. I thought that would be a great opportunity to explain our decision making. While the fans were watching the incident on the big screen or at home on TV, I could be talking them through it: 'Right, the defender has hit the attacker on the head, what we need to decide is whether it's a yellow or red card . . .'

But when I started to do exactly that, I was told, 'You're not there to commentate. And you're taking too long. Just give the yellow or red card and get on with the game.' I understood where they were coming from – they wanted to have as few stoppages as possible – but rugby is pretty bloody complicated, so I thought it was my job to commentate so that spectators understood my thought process. And if I got my explanation in early, I'd dictate how the conversation went in the actual commentary box, hopefully making the decision less controversial than it otherwise might have been.

It's funny in hindsight, because almost all rugby referees commentate now – and it's one of the few things we're applauded for – while one of the biggest criticisms of football's video assistant referee (VAR) is that nobody explains their decision making, and therefore nobody in the stadium or watching on TV knows how on earth some decisions are arrived at.

However, I'd never advise any young referee to follow the example of Didier Mené, despite him being a bit of a hero of mine.

Didier was one of France's top referees for quite a few years and one of the last mavericks, in that he spoke his mind and didn't care what anyone thought. I'm told that when Didier wasn't selected for the 1999 World Cup, he barged into a meeting of selectors and pointed at them one by one while saying, 'You are a shit, you are a shit, you are a shit,' before leaving the building. Funnily enough, he didn't referee many Tests after that (his most famous game was the second Test between the Lions and South Africa in 1997, when Jeremy Guscott kicked that last-gasp drop goal to clinch the series).

Didier was one of the first TMOs, if not the first. A mutual friend, David "Kurky" Kurk, who used to run touch in the Premiership, was on a sun lounger in Portugal, watching this game that Didier was TMO for, when there was a disputed try in the corner. The referee referred it and the commentator started talking things up – 'We're about to see rugby history being made with the very first TMO decision', that sort of thing. Anyway, Kurky decided he'd ring Didier, and was a tad surprised when Didier answered. Kurky asked, 'Aren't you supposed to be the TMO for this game?' And Didier replied, 'Yes. I am here now. So, Kurky, what do you think should be the decision?' Kurky said, 'Looks like a try to me,' and Didier replied, 'Looks like a try to me as well.' And he duly awarded it.

Then there was the time Didier was reffing a Championship game in England and I was his touch judge. A big fight broke out, Didier separated the players and gave both combatants a yellow card. As they were trudging off, one of them turned to Didier and said, 'Fuck you.' So Didier blew his whistle, called the bloke back and said, 'No, no, monsieur, I decide who fuck me, now I fuck you!' and showed him a red card. The bloke trudged off again, far more sheepish than before, and some of his teammates were openly laughing at Didier's sheer audacity.

Amazingly, Didier became head of French referees and had a lot of influence in the French Rugby Federation. Sadly, he passed away suddenly in 2023, but I'm glad to say his spirit lives on in the lower levels of the game. Recently, a good friend of mine reffed a game and afterwards a player from the losing team started giving him a load of grief. So my mate took his shirt off, asked the player if he wanted to take it any further, and the player scurried off.

I must admit I admired that. I thought, *Good for him. Why should he put up with that kind of nonsense?* And I thought the reaction of the player was very telling. When he abuses a referee, he expects him just to stand there and take it. But when a referee bites back, he runs away with his tail between his legs. Not that I ever thought about taking a similar stand. If I took my shirt off and asked a Premiership player if he wanted to take it further, the only damage I'd inflict is if the poor bloke laughed so much his sides split.

One of the biggest problems with referee managers is they flip-flop. Referees will receive an edict halfway through a tournament – 'Right, you've now got to start coming down hard on X, Y or Z' – and suddenly there will be this focus on an aspect of the game that most people didn't even notice was happening. And referees will become so preoccupied with following the new edict that they'll forget the fundamentals, such as refereeing the breakdown.

Some of the edicts that get passed down from World Rugby, as the IRB is now known, are just ridiculous. For example, I always got lambasted for using players' first names.

Initially, the reason they gave me was, 'You're not their mate, you're there to referee them.' I'd reply, 'I'm not trying to be their mate, I'm just trying to get them to listen to me.' In my office, I don't call people I work with 'secretary' or 'associate' or 'clerk', I call them by their first name, because that's the respectful thing to do. In the same way, it would be odd if a player called me 'Barnesy' and I called them 'number ten'.

Plus, in the midst of battle, I'll sometimes forget what number a player is. Is the lock who's just committed a foul and is now staring straight at me number four or number five? Or what about the replacement who's just come on? I might not know what number he is, but I will probably know his name.

Someone else said to me once, 'But you don't know all the players' first names, so using some and not others looks like favouritism.' When it comes to refereeing teams I don't know as well, that's a fair point. But what I'll do in that case is memorise three key players' first names from either side – usually the captain, hooker and scrum-half – and use them throughout.

Before Georgia v. Uruguay at the 2019 World Cup, I went into both sides' changing rooms, introduced myself to the skippers and had a little chat with them. When I needed a friend during the game, I was able to say, 'Jaba/ Juan Manuel, can I have a quick word . . .', instead of barking their number at them.

I was axed for the 2009 Six Nations for using first names – that's how seriously the bosses take it. I was still being reminded not to use first names during the 2023 Six Nations, but I never stopped because I do it for a good reason, not to be some kind of maverick.

Having been dropped in 2009, I was parachuted in when Steve Walsh got injured and pulled out of the Wales–Ireland game in Cardiff. (Steve was much maligned as a bit of a poser, but he was a bloody good ref.) So I'd gone from not even being on the bench to starting the biggest game of the tournament, which was indicative of the muddled thinking at the top.

That was the game when Ronan O'Gara gave Ireland the lead with a late, late drop goal, before I gave Wales a penalty in the dying seconds, after Paddy Wallace strayed offside (poor old Paddy went white as a sheet). Stephen Jones missed from just inside the Irish half and that was the last kick of the tournament, meaning Ireland had won their first Grand Slam since 1948. As for me, I was suddenly one of the best few referees in the world again.

After the game, there was a black-tie function at the Hilton. That was done and dusted by ten o'clock, but the Irish invited me along to the nightclub Tiger Tiger, where they'd booked a private room. I thought, *The Grand Slam-winning team want to take me out for a beer. Brilliant, I'll have some of that.*

However, a few minutes later, Wales captain Ryan Jones informed me that they also had a private room at Tiger

Tiger, except with a free bar. I spent most of the night in there instead, as did most of the Ireland team.

When Tiger Tiger kicked us all out at 1 a.m., Nigel Owens (my reserve ref that day), Adam Jones, Ryan Jones and I all headed to a gay nightclub called Club X, whose owner Nige knew. By 4 a.m., Adam Jones and I were scrummaging on the dancefloor with our tops off, and we all ended up getting chucked out.

I also got dropped after the 2012 Six Nations because the IRB had started analysing how much we penalised attack and defence, and discovered I'd only penalised attack at the breakdown once or twice in my last ten games.

I was letting things go, only giving a penalty if a defender had done something really well, because I thought that was the best way of allowing games to breathe and flow. But it wasn't a new approach on my part, I'd been reffing like that for years. I felt like saying, *How have you only just noticed?*

I thought that when attack was penalised too much, it made for a stodgier game. But because Ireland's Alain Rolland was penalising attack and defence 60–40, and he was the IRB's favourite, my stats made me look out of touch.

When they told me I was dropped, I said, 'Hold on, where's this come from? Can you show me which penalties you think I should have given that I didn't?' I even went back over all my old reports to see if anyone had raised it as a concern. Nobody had. I wouldn't have minded if they'd just told me they thought I was refereeing badly, but this just seemed like an excuse.

When I asked what I needed to do to get back in their good books, they replied, 'Penalise the attack more.' A few months later, I was brought off the naughty step and sent off to the Pacific Six Nations in Japan, to show that I'd learned. They even sent a retired Kiwi ref, the guy who had mentored the IRB's referee manager Paddy O'Brien, to keep an eye on me.

I'd normally be quite sociable on those kinds of trips, but I didn't have a drink for two weeks and trained every day. I also had a lot of chats with my Kiwi overseer about positioning and, you guessed it, penalising the attack.

My first game was Samoa v. Tonga in Nagoya and I awarded something like thirty penalties. My second game, Fiji v. Samoa in Tokyo, was much the same.

It wasn't as if I was making free kicks and penalties up, it was more the case that I was being very strict around grey areas I'd previously been loose on. For example, what is and what isn't side entry to a ruck is open to interpretation – does a player have to be ninety degrees to the touchline or eighty degrees? – but I was now being quite harsh. Before, someone would have needed to have had their arms wrapped around the ball, and probably be lifting the tackled player off the floor, before I gave a holding on penalty, but now I was penalising players for putting their fingertips on it, even for a split second.

Afterwards, the selectors said, 'Well done, you've listened.' Never mind that all that whistling had ruined the flow of those games, I'd tugged my forelock and said thank you enough to be welcomed back into the fold.

I flew straight to Argentina, where I ran touch for their two Tests against France. Ireland's George Clancy reffed both games, which I suspect was my boss's way of saying, *Don't get complacent, there are still referees doing the job better than you.* But a few months later, I was refereeing Australia v. Argentina in the Rugby Championship, as the Tri Nations had become. I guess that's what happens when you play the game, which is an awful phrase that makes me wince, because it essentially means you're not being yourself.

6

2007 and All That

The second international I refereed was Japan v. Fiji in Osaka, which was also part of the inaugural Pacific Nations Cup. There followed a World Cup qualifier between Romania and Georgia, an autumn international between Wales and the Pacific Islanders at the Millennium Stadium, before Italy v. France in 2007, which was my Six Nations debut.

I was sitting in my hotel room in Rome, thinking, *This is all a little bit odd. How have I ended up here?* Imposter syndrome had kicked in again. But that game went rather well. Some might say too well.

Probably because neither team knew what I was going to do, they decided not to compete at the breakdown (it's possible the French defence coach, Dave Ellis, had looked at my stats, seen I hardly ever penalised attack and said, 'Back off, because he's going to come down hard on you.').

Whatever the reason, every time a tackle was made, almost everyone stepped back and fanned out, like they do in rugby league, and I gave hardly any penalties, nine in total.

After the game, one of my touch judges, Dave Pearson, who had been officiating at that level for a few years already, said, 'Mate, for everyone to have behaved like that on your Six Nations debut, you must have golden balls.'

A few weeks after the Six Nations ended, I was named one of twelve referees for the 2007 World Cup in France, while Dave was only picked as a touch judge. That was extremely harsh on Dave. I'd only refereed a few internationals compared to him, and I was still in my twenties, but the IRB obviously thought I was one for the future.

A couple of months before the World Cup kicked off, I refereed my first Tri Nations game, between South Africa and Australia in Cape Town. A few months earlier, I was refereeing in front of a few thousand people at the Dinamo Stadium in Bucharest. Now, I was refereeing some of the greatest players on the planet, including Victor Matfield, John Smit and Schalk Burger for the Springboks, and George Smith, George Gregan and Stephen Larkham for the Wallabies, at the famous Newlands, which hosted its first Test in 1891.

I was already aware of how passionate Springbok fans could be because I'd toured South Africa with my university team in 2000. Our mascot was an inflatable pig, but she didn't last long. I was waving her about during the first Test between South Africa and England at Pretoria when a well-oiled local pulled out a twelve-inch Bowie knife and stabbed her to death. England lost that game, but I wasn't too disappointed about that.

But just as in the Italy–France game, both teams left me alone at Newlands. They'd obviously watched my previous games and thought, *There's no point attacking the breakdown, we'll just get pinged.* It was a straightforward, albeit close, game, but slightly surreal because there were all these very experienced players on the field and none of them tried it on.

My main memory of that game was the twenty-year-old François Steyn coming off the bench for the Boks and kicking two late drop goals to win it, the first from forty-odd metres out, right on the touchline. I was watching these kicks soar through the air, thinking, *Whoa, so this is what altitude does to the ball.* Then I remembered that Cape Town isn't at altitude.

I was the most junior of the World Cup refs by a country mile (the other two English refs, Whitey and Spreaders, were in their forties), and while I'm sure some of my colleagues were taken aback by my selection, I was only down to referee four fairly low-key group games, and I was sure I'd be jettisoned before the knockout stages.

My first game in France was New Zealand v. Italy in Marseille, and it was as one-sided as everyone expected, the All Blacks winning 76–14. On a morning stroll in my flip-flops, I kicked a kerb and broke my little toe the morning before my second game, Ireland v. Georgia in Bordeaux, but was desperate not to miss out, so I kept quiet, taped it up and limped through it. Ireland, who were a bit iffy that year, only just managed to win that one, and my other two group games were also unexpectedly tight affairs, with South Africa only just beating Tonga, who ran the Springboks ragged, and Samoa edging the United States.

After that Samoa–USA game, I thought my refereeing duties were over, and that I'd maybe get one or two more games running touch. That would have been fine by me – I thought I'd refereed well up to that point, but they weren't exactly high-profile matches. But when the twelve remaining officials were summoned to a meeting by the IRB's referee manager, things got a bit weird.

Alain Rolland was very experienced (and expected to get the nod for the final), so when he was announced as the man in charge of the England v. Australia quarter-final, there was a big round of applause. It was the same when Alain's Irish compatriot Alan Lewis (who had also refereed at the 2003 World Cup) was announced as the man in charge of South Africa v. Fiji, and when France's Joël Jutge (another 2003 World Cup veteran) was announced as the man in charge of Argentina v. Scotland. But when I was announced as the referee for France v. New Zealand – The Big One! – you could have heard a pin drop.

The overriding emotion in the room was shock, as if someone had let one rip at a funeral. I looked around at all these really impressive blokes like Whitey, Spreaders and Jonathan Kaplan, who was appearing in his third World Cup, and I had to stop myself from giggling. Compared to those guys, I hadn't really done anything.

Not that I was complaining. *Great,* I thought, *I'm refereeing the biggest game of the tournament so far. I'll invite all my friends and family along and afterwards we'll have a big celebration.*

Because France had finished second in their group behind Argentina, they were playing the All Blacks in Cardiff (the Pumas were playing Scotland in Paris). Whenever I refereed at the Millennium Stadium, my touch judges and I walked there from our hotel, the Hilton on Greyfriars Road, and the streets were always mayhem. But that night had an added layer of surrealism.

There were tens of thousands of Irish fans in town because they'd anticipated their team finishing second behind France (or Argentina) in their group. That meant the streets were awash with green rather than red. There were plenty of Kiwis, the All Blacks having romped through their group (averaging seventy-odd points per game), and even though far fewer French fans had managed to make the trip, they punched above their weight in terms of noise.

Once we'd made it into the ground, we got changed, chatted about who was doing what, checked the players' boots, and that was pretty much that. As I say, my approach was very different in those days.

The singing of the 'Marseillaise' is always emotional, but this time there were even more tears than usual. And because the roof was closed, it sounded like there were 50,000 French people in the stadium, rather than hundreds.

Both sides were meant to stand on their ten-metre lines during the haka but ended up almost nose to nose on the halfway. France back row Sébastian Chabal, a cult figure who looked and played like a caveman, was laughing in Ali Williams's face, while camera flashes went off all over the stadium.

I didn't think it was my place to separate them (before one game between Wales and New Zealand, the two teams stood staring at each other for about a minute after the haka was over, and when the referee jumped between them and tried to get them to move, they ignored him), but I thought, *Shit, this is gonna be a bit tasty . . .*

A few minutes in, French flanker Serge Betsen was knocked out trying to tackle Joe Rokocoko and had to be helped from the field. And there were huge cheers after I penalised All Blacks captain Richie McCaw (twice) for not rolling away at the tackle. But in terms of actual rugby, not a great deal happened in those first fifteen minutes or so, besides a lot of kicking and a Dan Carter penalty.

All Blacks centre Luke McAlister scored the first try of the match after seventeen minutes, and Carter popped over a conversion and another penalty. When France missed a couple of kicks at goal, there was a sense that the game was already slipping away from them, although Lionel Beauxis did nail a long-range penalty to make it 13–3 just before half-time.

I'd maintained a low-key presence for most of the first half because I had a basic philosophy, which was to allow teams to play, and the players had, for the most part, wanted to do that.

But you're very sensitive to momentum shifts as a referee. It might be a wonky bounce of a ball, which one team capitalises on, or a missed penalty attempt, which elicits groans from the crowd. Suddenly you're thinking, *Hmm, I've felt this before, might be time to strap ourselves in . . .*

This time it was a couple of French attacks just after the restart, which raised the volume significantly. Every neutral in that crowd wasn't neutral at all, they were all willing France to win. So when I sent McAlister to the sinbin for a body check on Yannick Jauzion, the crowd went wild. Then the Irish fans started singing 'The Fields of Athenry', which felt odd in the circumstances.

On fifty-four minutes, Carter tugged a drop goal wide and France hit the All Blacks on the counter, Thierry Dusautoir, who was heroic in defence that night, eventually touching down, before Beauxis kicked the conversion to make it 13–13. Suddenly, I was well and truly in the game, and acutely aware that the result might hinge on a decision I made – or didn't.

Carter limped off, closely followed by his replacement Nick Evans, but New Zealand took the lead again through a Rodney So'oialo try. Then it happened. French full-back Damien Traille burst through the line and offloaded to replacement fly-half Frédéric Michalak. Michalak sprinted into the New Zealand twenty-two, slowed up, pirouetted and passed to Jauzion, who dived over to make it 18–18. When Jean-Baptiste Élissalde kicked the extras, the noise was ear-splitting.

Not that it felt like the All Blacks were dead and buried, because there were still twenty-one minutes to play. But for reasons I will never understand, they stopped playing with width and kept battering down the middle instead, with constant pick and goes. I'd never seen them play that way, and it was great for the French because that's how it was every week in the Top 14, attackers and defenders smashing into each other around the goal-line.

The closer we got to the final whistle, the more I sensed fear in the All Black ranks because they weren't making many dents in the French defence. As for me, I wasn't thinking anything other than, *Just keep letting the game flow.*

As my career progressed, and I gained more experience of refereeing close games in big tournaments, I became more aware that I might have to make a decision that would decide the outcome of the match, and of the fallout that might follow. But back then, I had no concept of what that might mean. There was still a part of me that couldn't believe I was on the field in the first place.

Eventually, McAlister, who had been moved to fly-half, was reduced to trying a drop goal from the halfway line – the All Blacks almost never kicked drop goals – and when it fell well short of the posts, that was that.

As I made my way from the pitch, I thought it had all gone quite well. I'd given hardly any penalties (France didn't give any away in the second half, which was remarkable), let things flow, and it had been an exciting game. But we were doing what we call our hot debrief in the changing room when Whitey, the TMO, popped his head around the door and said, 'There might have been a forward pass in the lead-up to one of France's tries, but we're not sure if it's that clear.'

When I saw the pass, from Traille to Michalak in the lead-up to France's second try, it was clearly forward. The TMO protocol was different back then, in that it wasn't used for possible forward passes, and there's no way I could have seen if it was forward from where I was standing. But none of that mattered. We'd allowed the try to stand, so it was going to be a headline.

We'd normally walk back to the hotel after a game in Cardiff, but this time we thought it made sense to get a lift. It was 10.30, there were a lot of pissed people about – many of them Kiwis – so we didn't want to risk it.

The roads were closed for another hour, so we decided to get some beers in and sit things out in the changing room. I was just finishing my first bottle when Spreaders, who had run touch, walked in and announced he'd sorted a ride. I thought he meant he'd arranged a car and special permission to use the roads, but he'd actually arranged a ride in an ambulance – Spreaders used to be a paramedic and had called in a favour from one of his old mates.

The French team were also staying at the Hilton, so there were French fans all over the steps leading up to the foyer, swigging from bottles, singing and chanting, waving tricolours, waiting for their heroes to arrive. Our ambulance had its blues and twos on, so they quietened down a bit and parted when we turned up, probably because they thought someone had taken ill. But when the doors opened and I jumped out with my two touch judges and the TMO, a huge cheer went up. They were patting us on the back, draping scarves around our necks, trying to kiss us. I remember thinking, *They must think international referees travel everywhere in the back of ambulances.*

Social media was still in its infancy in 2007 and most websites had still only published on-the-whistle reports, so I still had no idea how big this headline was going to be when I finally fell into bed, at about six in the morning. I awoke to knocking on my door and assumed it was room service, wanting to clean my room. I told them to come back later, but whoever it was knocked again. I dragged myself out of bed, opened the door, and there was a bloke standing there. 'Hello, Wayne,' he said. 'I'm from the *New Zealand Herald.*'

When his article appeared, it read something along the lines of, 'I was greeted by a half-naked, bleary-eyed Wayne Barnes, who had clearly just got out of bed at 11 a.m.' He obviously wanted people to think I was so depressed about my performance that I was hiding myself away from the world.

I got plenty of stick from the New Zealand media, some of which was a bit much. But the abuse on internet message boards and Facebook, which had just taken off, was on a whole different level. Groups were set up dedicated to slagging me off, and while the stuff about me being French and a cheat was like water off a duck's back, the death threats jarred a bit.

One Facebook group was called 'WAYNE BARNES MUST DIE'. Apparently, my Wikipedia page had been turned into a mock obituary even before the final whistle. I thought, *Fair enough, I missed a forward pass, but I'm not sure I deserve to be bumped off because of it.*

Things got sillier and sillier. I was mentioned in the New Zealand parliament. I was voted third most hated man in New Zealand, after Osama bin Laden and Saddam Hussein, who were responsible for tens of thousands of deaths between them. They burned an effigy of me in Christchurch, and in Cowboys bar in Queenstown, they placed a bust of my head in a urinal, accompanied by the sign: PISSED OFF IN CARDIFF? PISSED ON IN QUEENSTOWN! (*The Times* rugby writer Stephen Jones, who always gets up Kiwi noses, was in a urinal in the other corner.) They only got rid of it a few years ago, when they installed a bust of Donald Trump instead. (Stephen was still there.)

It didn't help that the IRB's referee manager, Paddy O'Brien, was a Kiwi and I believe didn't know how to react to the situation. He defended me in interviews, but made a crass comment along the lines of, 'The New Zealand public and press just need to grow up,' which stoked the flames.

Usually, one of the referees' selectors would do the post-match review, but on this occasion, all four of them did it. I've still got that review somewhere, and it's really positive. But it felt as if Paddy, and another selector who was also a Kiwi, found it very difficult to talk to me, let alone make any suggestions as to how to improve as a referee or deal with the situation.

A lot of New Zealand fans flew in for the semi-finals and final (that's how confident New Zealand fans were of success), so when I arrived back at my hotel in Paris, three coach loads of them were checking in. That was a bit hairy, and I didn't spend much time there for the rest of the tournament.

When some mates turned up for the game between France and England, they decided I'd have to attend the game in disguise because 20,000 Kiwi fans were expected, and some of them might well have bristled at my presence. They stuck a platinum-blonde wig, fake moustache and giant sunglasses on me, nicknamed me Jimmy Barnes, and off we went to the Stade de France.

As Jimmy Barnes, and with a few drinks inside me, I managed to have a grand evening. That's what mates are good for, taking the piss and making you realise it's just a game of rugby, not life and death. I even saw the funny side when some Kiwi fans I got chatting to started slagging Wayne Barnes off. 'Wayne Barnes is an idiot,' I told them, as deadpan as it's possible to be while wearing a platinum-blonde wig, fake moustache and giant sunglasses.

A few months after the 2007 World Cup, I was chatting to my coach Brian Campsall, who was also an international referee. He said to me, 'There's no way you should have done that game,' and I was affronted. I said to him, 'How dare you? I was reffing as well as anyone in the tournament, and I reffed that game well apart from that bloody forward pass.' Campo replied, 'It was just the wrong game for you. You didn't need it at that stage in your career. If they really wanted to give you one, why not South Africa v. Fiji? You'd still have experienced a big knockout game, but it would have been far less of a risk.'

I was really shitty with Campo, and we didn't leave on great terms. I kept thinking, *What the hell does he know about it?* But as time went on, I realised he was right. I asked myself, *I know the law book, but do I know the game?* Of course I didn't know the game, and of course I wasn't ready. True, I had performed well in my pre-World Cup games, but I think I'd got lucky because teams erred on the side of caution, instead of trying to test me.

I compared the situation to my legal career. A law firm wouldn't give its biggest, most complex brief to a young, junior lawyer, however promising. That would be crass and irresponsible because that big, complex case might damage them irreparably, and scupper what might have been a fine career. In hindsight, giving me that quarter-final was a ridiculous appointment.

I only discovered the clashing irony of the whole situation a few years later, when someone let slip that the IRB had asked the All Blacks who they'd like to referee that game. They'd suggested me.

Presumably, head coach Graham Henry wanted a referee who would let the game flow because they were a very attack-minded team.

In 2012, Henry brought out his autobiography, in which he wondered if I'd been involved in match-fixing. Someone that senior and with that much influence saying something like that is pretty shitty and could have had huge ramifications for me and the game of rugby. I can forgive someone saying something horrible in the heat of the moment, but he'd had five years to think about it, and an editor must have said to him at some point, 'Do you really want to write that?'

Some libel lawyers I knew asked if I'd be interested in suing, but it wasn't a guaranteed win and it would have put my name in the headlines when I just wanted to stay in the background, so I decided against it. I've never shaken Henry's hand since, though, and I doubt I ever will.

Hot on the heels of Henry's memoir was Richie McCaw's, and he dredged the whole episode up again. McCaw said I'd been 'frozen with fear' and 'wouldn't make any big calls' because I was so inexperienced. Besides the forward pass, I'm not sure what 'big calls' he thought I should have made.

The Kiwis just wouldn't let it lie. In 2016, I officiated Wales's series in New Zealand, and before the second Test in Wellington, I went to a Welsh bar to watch England v. Wales in the football European Championship.

I was with Welsh rugby legend Ieuan Evans, and the owner got him to sign and write a comment in their guestbook. When they asked me to do the same, I said I had nothing to say. They suggested I write, 'Sorry about the forward pass', and I politely declined. But they kept badgering me, and I eventually wrote, 'What pass?' The next day, there was a story about me in the *New Zealand Herald*, claiming I still wasn't taking knocking them out of the 2007 World Cup seriously.

I'm glad to say this chapter has a happy ending. In 2017, I refereed a Bledisloe Cup game in Auckland. Afterwards, someone knocked on my changing-room door and said I had a visitor. I was stark-bollock naked, so I quickly put on a tracksuit top and wrapped a towel around my waist, before New Zealand Prime Minister Jacinda Arden was ushered in.

I've got a lovely photo of Jacinda and me chatting away, but I do wonder whether someone said to her, 'Maybe you should bury the hatchet, for the sake of diplomacy,' which just shows the importance of rugby to that country.

he Barnes brothers at my
ondon-based stag do at
psom races in July 2013.
he first stag do took place
mmediately after the 2013
remiership final.

The unbeaten Whitecross
U-15 rugby team with me in
the back row and David 'Lardy'
Emery, the mastermind
behind the Forest v. Barnes
annual charity match, in the
middle row.

5s team. Back row: Lee Johnson, Ross Nelmes, Matthew James, Brett Scriven (captain), Wayne
nes, Nathan Jeynes. Middle Row: Dale Wicks, Daniel Emery, John Cooke, Ricky Gunter, Robert
t. Front row: Charles Vine, Edwin Ramos, David Hartwell, Scott James,

Gloucestershire cup match
ween Cheltenham and Clifton
d the Prince of Wales Stadium
h John Hackett running touch
d me donning some impressive
rt shorts.

One of the many main university haircuts me and my mates thought were a good idea. Uncle Ivan, Danny Williams and Candle seemed to have got away without having to bleach their hair

Our victorious Norfolk Plate university team having just beaten Crusaders.

The Norfolk Plate being returned to me by Rodders, a long serving UEA prop, the day after receiving my honorary doctorate. You'll see it's lost its shine.

Me and Polly moments before receiving my honorary doctorate in July 2016.

The toss before Uruguay and Georgia at Kumagaya Stadium. (© Clive Rose-World Rugby/ Getty images)

Johnny Lacey and I in Japan on my 'rehabilitation' tour of 2012.

Our university rugby team on tour to SA in 2000. You'll notice the inflatable pig has already been slain.

The England refereeing contingent of Chris White, Dave Pearson, Tony Spreadbury and me, days prior to RWC 2007.

In the back of an ambulance on the way home from the Millennium Stadium following the 2007 quarter-final when France beat New Zealand.

A banner at an All Blacks game months after the 2007 quarter-final.

The famous urinal in the Cowboys Bar in Queenstown, New Zealand. 'Pissed off in Cardiff? Pissed on in Queenstown!'

My undercover outfit following the quarter-final loss by New Zealand. Bruno and Ox obviously thought long and hard about the disguise.

Me and Jacinda in the Eden Park changing room following the Bledisloe Cup match in 2018.

My last Premiership final in 2022 with Christophe Ridley and Luke Pearce having my back for this game. (© Kate Saddler)

Craig Joubert and I following the 2011 RWC quarter-final match between Wales and Ireland in Wellington.

Me and Polly trying to get some peace and quiet in Cathedral Cove.

Me with the wig and gown my Nanny Moaner bought me, standing within the grounds of Lincoln's Inn.

The twelve referees and Joël Jutge at Westminster Abbey in the lead up to RWC 2015.

Nigel and I share a wry smile before the 2015 RWC final between New Zealand and Australia.

Receiving our medals from Prince Harry and King Jason.

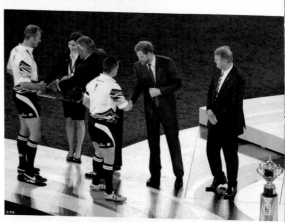

The Rugby World Cup final team of match officials standing on the Twickenham pitch prior to kick off.

7

Obsession

Having concluded that I didn't understand rugby as well as I thought I did, and that my freak factor was no longer working, I decided to get some people around me who knew the game back to front.

Up to that point, I'd only been coached by other referees, but I now thought I needed input from people who worked in different disciplines, including actual rugby coaches.

Phil Keith-Roach is a former hooker who played for Cambridge University in three Varsity games, captained Rosslyn Park for years, and was England's scrum coach when they won the World Cup. I bumped into Roachy at an RFU event and we got on well, so I asked if he'd help with my game preparation. The scrum is one of the most difficult areas to referee, and for everyone to understand, but I thought if Roachy could tell me how teams were going to scrummage and the particular challenges I might face, I'd at least know what was going on.

Roachy and I would meet in restaurants and bars near his house in Maida Vale, west London. We'd spend hours looking at different scrums: how players set up when they're in a strong position, what happens when they get tired, who's cheating and how. Tables and chairs would be pushed aside in some Italian joint and Roachy would scrummage me around the place, saying stuff like, 'This bind really hurts,' or 'This is why he might put his head at this angle rather than that angle.' It was forensic, while also being a lot of fun.

Now, I could say to coaches before a game, 'Look, I've prepared with my scrum coach, Phil Keith-Roach, and this is what I think will help. If you can sort these things out, I'll be able to stay out of the way.' Because staying out of the way was all I ever wanted to do. I didn't want to be one of those pernickety referees who was constantly blowing their whistle, I wanted to get teams to iron out their own faults early so that people didn't see, hear or mention me. If they didn't see, hear or mention me, that normally meant a good game of rugby had been played, and I'd soon be refereeing another good game of rugby.

I have worked with Roachy for sixteen years. We meet before every big international and major European club fixture. Before the Champions Cup semi-final between Leinster and Toulouse in 2023, we pored over scrums for three or four hours. After games, we'd do a review, asking what we did and didn't get right. And when a coach would tell me I'd got certain things wrong, and I'd tell them I didn't agree, we'd both know that Roachy was on my side. Everyone knows Roachy, he's got huge credibility, which gave me more credibility.

I started to take my physical preparation more seriously: eat better, drink less, train more. Yes, I was probably a little bit unlucky in that World Cup quarter-final, in that it was a quick breakout by France that led to the controversial try, but the fitter you are as a ref, the less likely you are to get caught out of position.

I also started to analyse teams more, working out where they tended to kick or attack from, which in turn meant I'd be able to anticipate where to be on the field at any given time, which in turn meant I wasn't having to bust a gut sprinting all the time.

It always amazed me that World Rugby never provided us refs with the full-time support of a psychologist, someone just to check in from time to time and see how we were doing. Blokes are terrible at talking about things, but I always thought it would be great if we were able to speak with a psychologist and say, 'I've been away for months, I'm getting a bit of grief from my partner, and I'm feeling a bit shit about it.'

Following an opportunity to listen to a well-known sports psych, I decided I would begin working with a sports-pscyh at my own expense, hoping it might be able to improve my game.

I listened to psychiatrist Steve Peters, who worked with British Cycling for years as well as Liverpool FC, the England football team and Ronnie O'Sullivan, and thought he made a lot of sense. He spoke about how football referees tend to protect the underdog, so that if a team is being well beaten, they'll start making decisions in their favour. The problem being, the team that were three goals down are suddenly one goal down, and they've got the momentum.

He also spoke about referees wanting to belong to the pack, which explains why fans are always complaining about home-town decisions. Referees aren't consciously biased, but they can be swayed by 80,000 screaming fans at Twickenham or Wembley without even knowing it.

But while being aware of that kind of psychological stuff makes certain things easier to accept and move on from, there have been points in my career where I've gone too far the other way, because I wanted to show I wasn't swayed by the home team's fans and could make a big decision against them. That big decision might have been right, but maybe I didn't need to make it.

You referee best when you've got a clear mind, when you see something and react to it without even thinking. As soon as you start 'layering', as I call it, thinking stuff like, *I gave that penalty earlier on, so now I've got to give the other team this one*, or *I've yellow-carded that team, I could do with finding an opportunity to yellow card the other team*, or *I wonder what the selectors will think*, you become vulnerable, and your decision making goes awry.

While my thinking got clearer as my career progressed, I was never completely immune to those kinds of thoughts. But having spoken to my sports psychologist about it, I started to write 'reset' on my hand, so that whenever I started drifting into that vulnerable zone, worrying about what other people were thinking – commentators, journalists, fans, coaches, selectors – I'd look at my hand and refocus.

The eagle-eyed among you might have seen me doing it and smiling, because I was thinking, *It doesn't matter how long I've been doing this, my mind still wanders . . .*

The biggest challenge for a rugby referee isn't how fast or fit they can get, or how easily they can get along with people, or even how well they know the law book, it's the psychological battle going on between their ears.

I also started to use my wife Polly as a bit of a sounding board, because your partner is likely to know you better than anyone else.

At the start of my international career, I'd always try to show I was happy before a match, which meant lots of big smiles and enthusiastic handshakes. But Polly said to me, 'You look deranged. People don't want to see you enjoying the occasion, they want to see that you're taking things seriously. If you walked into a courtroom and the judge was grinning like a Cheshire cat, you'd think he was being weird and inappropriate, so why are you doing it on the rugby field?'

The counter argument is that it's not a courtroom, it's a game of rugby. But Polly wasn't suggesting I look solemn, as if it was a matter of life and death, she was just suggesting I stopped looking like I was trying to please everyone. I don't always take Polly's advice well at first – 'What do you know about rugby?' – but I usually have to concede that it makes sense.

A few years ago, I was refereeing Wales v. Ireland and Johnny Sexton went down injured. I always tried to keep my distance from the teams during stoppages to stop players trying to get in my ear. But on this occasion, Ken Owens wandered over and asked something about the scrums, before moving on to general chitchat.

He asked how my Christmas was, I told him I'd spent time with the family, and that was pretty much the extent of it. But when Ken wandered off again, Ireland lock James Ryan came over and said, 'What were you talking to him about?' I replied, 'Well, actually, Christmas.' Sounds innocuous, and it was, but it was picked up by my microphone and the following day there was a comment in the press along the lines of, 'Johnny Sexton was being treated for an injury and Wayne Barnes was going on about Christmas.' Polly made me understand that it didn't sound good, even though I hadn't meant any offence.

Polly also intervened when Specsavers wanted to do some content with me. I thought it could be quite amusing, like when Gareth Southgate, Stuart Pearce and Chris Waddle did that Pizza Hut advert in 1996, making fun of the fact they'd all missed penalties for England in major tournaments. But Polly was having none of it. Her attitude was, 'How dare they? Do you realise that would be taking the piss out of you?' We had a few arguments about it, and I eventually saw that Polly was right. Again.

A few years later, Specsavers' logo started appearing on referees' shirts. I still saw the funny side, but it reinforced my belief that the authorities didn't have our backs. Essentially, it was a sponsorship deal that took the piss out of referees, and nobody had put their hand up and said, *You know what, this doesn't sit right with me.* Or maybe they had, and nobody listened.

I've had a few mentors in my time, in both the legal and rugby worlds, but no one has had a bigger impact on my life than Nigel Yates. Which is strange, in a way, because when we first met, I thought he was an obnoxious, posh twat.

Nigel, who was a regular in the Premiership, was refereeing a game at North Walsham for some reason, and I was doing the seconds or thirds match. He turned up in a convertible Mercedes, looking immaculate in a shirt and tie, and I turned up in a mate's clapped-out VW, looking exactly like what I was: a broke student whose bedroom floor doubled as a wardrobe. He looked at me as if to say, *What the hell have we got here?* While I thought, *What an arrogant knobhead.*

But Nigel and I soon got to know each other properly and he ended up being my coach. Nigel holds people to account (which is probably why he was so aghast at my appearance when he first laid eyes on me) and is very good at calling out bullshit, which is why he was so useful as a sounding board.

Nigel lives up in Manchester, so if I was doing a Sale game, I'd go straight from the ground to Nigel's house. We would open the bottle of wine I'd brought along at about ten o'clock, sit down at the big wooden table he had in his kitchen and start chatting about rugby and life in general. Nigel was a lawyer like me, so we had a lot in common, and some of those chats would go on until 3 a.m. Luckily, he had a very good wine cellar, so once my bottle was polished off, we'd get stuck into some of his really good stuff.

Nigel wasn't really into the technical side of rugby but was a brilliant people person. After the 2011 World Cup, I came home very disillusioned with rugby, what with everything that had gone on in New Zealand (I'll go into more detail later). I even thought I might be done with it. But one of my first games back was up in Newcastle, and my referee manager asked Nigel to come up and meet me. Nigel is a grumpy so and so who hates staying away from home, but he sat with me until 2 a.m. And when I told him how down I was, he said to me, 'Stop being a spoilt twat. Just show them how good you can be and stick two fingers up at them.'

That conversation was a pivotal moment in my life, because after that I knuckled down, got better and squeezed another twelve years out of the game. Whenever I was feeling down about rugby, I'd phone Nigel and get his thoughts. Sometimes he'd tell me I was being precious, sometimes he'd tell me I was right and had been hard done by. Either way, it was never a catastrophe in Nigel's eyes. And if I had good news to share, like when I was picked for a World Cup, Nigel would be the first person I called after my wife.

My pre-match preparation having been almost non-existent when I started refereeing professional rugby – even before the 2007 World Cup quarter-final between France and New Zealand, it wouldn't have been much more than a chat with my team – it became something I took a lot of pride in, almost an obsession.

It wasn't possible to prepare exactly the same way for every game, because it would depend on how much footage I could get hold of. But before a big club game or an international, I'd get to see all the teams' scrums and lineouts from their previous however many games, all their kick-offs, how the nines exit, how the tens exit. I'd also look at penalty stats – where each side gives them away, which players give them away.

As well as Roachy, I'd speak to an international coach (obviously someone who wasn't connected to either team) and he'd take me through expected game plans: where do they kick from, where do they kick to, where do they attack from, if they have a habit of pre-latching before making contact (which is when three or more attacking players bind together, effectively forming a flying wedge).

It was all about building a picture of how teams played, and what the game might look like – almost like creating a simulation in my head – so I was less likely to see something I'd never seen before and get spooked. Because a spooked referee – a spooked anyone – is more likely to get things wrong.

It was the same when I was a young barrister. Once I'd been around the block a few times and run the gamut of cases, I knew what to expect most of the time. Sometimes, something odd would come up, which would have me scrambling around for the right answer, but I'd prepare for all sorts of weird scenarios, just as I prepared for all sorts of weird scenarios in rugby.

Of course, sometimes things happen that are almost impossible to prepare for, like when two Just Stop Oil protestors ran on to the pitch and threw paint powder during the 2023 Premiership final. All Luke Pearce could do was stop the game and hope security would do what they had to do. But I have thought about what I'd do if a streaker ran on the field and grabbed the ball (even though there probably hasn't been a streaker at Twickenham since Erika Roe in 1982).

People will accuse me of pre-judging, but every elite sportsperson in the world will analyse opponents before a game and say, 'This is what I'll do if they do that, this is what I'll do if they do this.' Seeing as much as you can before you step on to the field takes some of the pressure off and enables you to perform consistently.

If it's an international, we'll do all our prep as a team the day before the game. We'll sit around a table, work out what the key areas are and agree on how we're going to handle them. On the morning of the game, we'll remind ourselves of those key areas and often do some role-play, which involves showing a couple of big-decision moments – red cards, tries in the corner – and talking through who should do what. Who leads the discussion? What is the TMO going to say? Who's making sure I haven't got the captain screaming and shouting at me? Who's making sure we haven't missed anything in the background? It's all just to get our minds working in game mode.

I like to be done and dusted by 10 a.m., after which I'll have a coffee and go for a walk. Often the French games kick off at 9 p.m., so if Polly's with me, I'll walk around Montmartre about six times, because she'll have said, 'I'm not staying in this beautiful city and sitting around in a hotel room all day.' To be fair to Polly, it's a nice way to switch off from rugby for a few hours.

I'll arrive at the ground a couple of hours before kick-off and look at some of the clips again to remind me of what I might see. And I'll also spark up an app I've got on my phone, which gets your eyes working more efficiently. It sounds odd, but eyegym.com really does work.

An hour before kick-off, the assistant refs will do the boot check, which is an opportunity to have a quick chat and reiterate the stuff I'd already told their coaches on the Tuesday. For example, if the backs have a habit of breaking the lineout early, I might get one of my assistants to remind them about that. It's just human nature that if you tell someone something once, they'll be able to convince themselves they didn't hear it or they forgot. But if you tell them two or three times, they won't have that excuse.

While the assistant refs are doing their thing, the referee will be doing the front-row briefing, which consists of final reminders and players asking a couple of key questions, usually things they have been told by their coaches.

When I was assistant referee for Scotland v. Ireland in the 2023 Six Nations, we were hanging around in the corridor before kick-off and one of the Scottish management team said, 'Are you coming in now?' It was five minutes before the scheduled time, but we thought we might as well get it out of the way.

We did the boot checks, referee Luke Pearce chatted to the front row, and all went smoothly. But ten minutes later, we got a message saying we'd have to go back, because Scotland head coach Gregor Townsend hadn't been there. So back we traipsed to the Scotland changing room, where we did exactly the same as before, except this time with Gregor watching and listening. I could hear Luke saying to the front row, 'Right, in case you'd forgotten . . .'

I've had the same whistle since that very first game between Bream Third XV and Berry Hill Wappers, while my tossing coin, which is an old penny with Queen Victoria on it, was given to me by one of my first referee coaches. In some of the bigger games, someone who's won a competition will present a special commemorative coin to the ref and have a picture taken, but most of the time I use my trusty old penny. Occasionally, I'll hand it over to one of the skippers and they'll say to me, 'What the hell is this, Barnesy?'

Talking of coins, former South African referee Mark Lawrence was also a magician, so he could do all sorts of tricks with them. At the 2007 World Cup, Mark, Craig Joubert and I caught a train down to Marseille together, and Mark did tricks all the way there. He was making coins disappear into thin air, swallowing balloons, bending spoons, making playing cards levitate. It was proper Paul Daniels stuff, and Craig and I were completely transfixed.

Before one Bledisloe Cup game, Mark made a coin disappear in mid-air during the toss. Apparently, Wallabies captain George Gregan was not impressed. 'Mate,' he said, 'you're here to do a job, not be a fucking comedian.' The following year, before another Bledisloe Cup game, Mark flipped the coin and it didn't come down again. Gregan was fuming and said to him, 'Mate, I told you last time, you're not a fucking comedian.' But this time, Mark hadn't made it disappear. It had got stuck in the rafters.

8

Fear and Loathing

I'm certainly not the only rugby referee who's been put through the wringer and let down by our bosses. At the 2011 World Cup, Bryce Lawrence got a load of abuse, including death threats, after Australia beat South Africa in the quarter-finals.

South African media and fans thought Wallaby back row David Pocock had got away with murder at the breakdown, and that Bryce, who's a Kiwi, was desperate for the All Blacks to avoid the Springboks in the semis, which was, of course, nonsense.

Bryce retired from refereeing the following year, blaming political pressure. Senior figures had kicked up a big fuss about his performance in that quarter-final, and subsequently he was dropped from the referees' roster.

At the 2015 World Cup, it was my old mate Craig Joubert's turn. I had tickets for the quarter-final between Scotland and Australia, which Craig was in charge of, but it was pouring down and I had a bit of a hangover following my quarter-final between Wales and South Africa the day before, so I gave them to a mate and watched it at home.

It was a very exciting match-up, and when Scotland centre Mark Bennett scored an interception try with seven minutes to go, it looked like the underdogs had pulled off a famous upset. But in the dying seconds, Scotland had a lineout, the ball was knocked forward and caught by Scottish hands, and Craig blew his whistle for offside. My gut feeling was that Craig had got it right, but when I saw the replays, which showed that the ball had come off a Wallaby player, I thought, *Oh shit, Craig is in trouble.*

He wasn't allowed to use the TMO to change his decision, so we had the absurd situation of everyone in the stadium having seen the replays on the big screen and knowing the decision was wrong, and Craig not being able to rectify it. Aussie fly-half Bernard Foley kicked the three points, meaning Australia won 35–34, and after blowing the final whistle, Craig ran straight off the field.

There was the inevitable media pile-on, with Craig being hammered for the decision itself and for apparently running from the scene of his crime. Scottish great Gavin Hastings said he was 'disgusted', and former England scrum-half Matt Dawson called him 'a disgrace' and said he should never referee another game. Remember, they were talking about a vastly experienced ref who was in charge of the 2011

World Cup final. To make things worse, World Rugby's chief executive suggested in an interview that Craig might have been 'keen to get to the bathroom'.

But I knew exactly what Craig was doing, because I'd done it myself. He knew he'd just made a controversial decision, and that Scottish players and coaches were going to be mad at him, so he wanted to get off the pitch as quickly as possible so that any altercations didn't take place in full view of the public, which would have further damaged the image of the game. Craig actually did have a conversation with Scotland head coach Vern Cotter in the tunnel – and as you can imagine, that got pretty heated – but it was Craig trying to protect the game, which I thought was smart on his part.

Things turned political very quickly, as they did with me after the 2007 World Cup. Craig was eventually handed a few draft statements, none of which he was happy with. As he rightly pointed out, World Rugby never made statements about refereeing decisions. But they went ahead and issued one anyway, saying he'd got it wrong and should have awarded Australia a scrum instead.

Craig thought he'd been chucked under a bus and went undercover for the rest of the tournament, rarely coming out of his hotel room. He did come out for the final referees' gathering, but only because he'd been assured we had a private room in a dimly lit Italian restaurant in Soho.

Craig was obviously disappointed he hadn't got the decision right, but he also knew his hands had been tied.

If you watch the incident back, the ball did take a small deflection off a Wallaby hand, but it's not easy to see, and Craig only had one angle and one take, unlike everyone watching the replays in the ground. It's a great example of how the media can turn a very understandable mistake by a referee into a calamitous, potentially career-ending blunder, and of how not to handle things as a governing body.

Things hadn't improved by the 2019 World Cup in Japan. That opening weekend had a couple of wrong decisions, including some missed red cards and a ton of TMO referrals. One of those games was France's narrow win over Argentina, in which a couple of calls went against the Pumas – and it just so happened that the vice-chair of World Rugby was former Pumas captain Agustín Pichot.

On the Sunday evening, us match officials got a text saying we had to attend a meeting the following morning at 8 a.m. And at this meeting, referee manager Alain Rolland announced that World Rugby was releasing a statement saying the refereeing hadn't been good enough so far. I put my hand up and said, 'I haven't refereed yet, so can they at least include a footnote saying, "Except for Wayne"?'

It probably wasn't the time for humour, and the group were rightly pretty pissed off. Lots of comments flew around the room, along the lines of, 'We're subcontracted to World Rugby for this tournament, we're part of their team, so why are they not sticking up for us?' 'What are World Rugby trying to achieve by making such a statement?' 'Would the All Blacks coaching staff allow the NZRU to make such a statement?' 'And why has our referee manager allowed it?'

It felt like World Rugby was making things up as it went along. Why did it not have a blanket policy that it would never comment on refereeing, instead of staying quiet sometimes and only releasing statements when it was expedient for certain people? From that point on, it felt like it was us against World Rugby, rather than us being part of the World Rugby team.

People in rugby are always going on about the sport's 'values' and 'integrity', but as soon as it gets a bit too hot in the kitchen, the people in charge start slagging off the refs. That's why I'm quite careful when I speak about football, because I don't agree that rugby is a morally superior game.

One of Nigel Owens's catchphrases is, 'This isn't soccer,' by which he means rugby players should behave differently to footballers. But as several football referees have pointed out to me, while they do have players diving in the tackle, and speaking back to them, they don't have players biting each other's ears, grabbing each other's nuts and trying to take each other's heads off, not to mention all the everyday cheating that goes on in scrums and rucks. And at least in football the people in charge have the referees' backs.

In February 2023, World Rugby announced it had commissioned a Netflix-style documentary series focusing on rugby referees. They said it would raise our profile, humanise us and show the public what a difficult job we had. It was a good idea in theory, but we wanted to know more detail. Would we get editorial rights? Would we be able to opt out altogether? Would we see any money? All stuff players and coaches would naturally ask.

World Rugby said it would get back to us, but the day before we travelled to our pre-World Cup camp, we got an email from our boss, telling us to expect a film crew at Toulouse Airport, who would be following us around for a few days.

The group of match officials were having conversations all that weekend and ended up on a call with World Rugby. We reiterated our concerns, and they told us they assumed we were all okay with it and were going to push ahead with filming regardless.

At the time of writing, I don't know what's happening and we are a week away from the tournament starting. But I'm not at all happy at the possibility of being filmed half-cut dancing on a table, which I've been known to do, because while I'm retiring from refereeing, I'm still a lawyer.

World Rugby already has a programme called *Whistle Watch*, hosted by Nigel Owens, in which he analyses the week's controversial refereeing decisions. Worse, he'll be doing it throughout the World Cup. I don't blame Nige for doing it, but I can't think of another governing body that would allow it. It certainly doesn't happen in football, cricket or rugby league.

When it was first aired, there was no interaction between Nige and the referee management, and in some cases, Nige would say a referee should have given a yellow card when the referee had already been told by his management that the red card he gave was the correct decision. And imagine the headlines if Nige comes out and says I got something wrong in a big game. I'm pretty sure it will be something along the lines of, 'Nigel Owens slams Barnes decision', because Nige is a big and credible name.

And recently, European Professional Club Rugby (EPCR), the body that organises the Champions and Challenge Cups, proposed the idea of posting controversial clips on its social media accounts, and getting people to vote on whether the referees got the decisions right or wrong. Then, at the end of the week, they would post a video of the referee manager giving his opinion.

World Rugby and the EPCR would argue that they just want to be more interactive, engaging and transparent, but when the digital agency they proposed the idea to asked for my view on it, I thought, *Who on earth thinks a governing body holding referees up to ridicule is a good idea? These people are meant to be upholding the values of the game.*

Before the start of the 2022–23 Premiership season, I said to the RFU, 'If you think I'm the best-performing referee, then pick me for the biggest games. If there are referees performing better than me, I don't expect any favours just because I've been doing it a long time.'

A few weeks before the last round of the regular season, I was told I was going to referee the final at Twickenham. I was chuffed because it showed I was still at the top of my game. I even arranged for a few people who had helped me during my career to come down for a few beers, plus my family. We could have all walked to the ground together, which would have been special.

But on the Monday before the semi-final, I was called out of the blue and told that because I was already doing the European Challenge Cup final, and they wanted to divvy the games up, I wasn't doing the Premiership final, I was doing the semi between Leicester and Sale instead.

I was more than irritated about it. If they'd said to me, 'Wayne, you're not doing the final because we've decided so and so will do a better job,' I'd have been disappointed but understanding. But they had said they were going to give the biggest games to the best performers, they'd told me I was the best performer, and now everything had changed at the last moment. Instead of me and my family walking down the road to Twickenham for my last Premiership game, I was going to have to arrange for them all to get up to Salford in five days' time.

I said to the RFU, 'Think back to when you were playing. You've reached a final, and a couple of weeks before the game, your head coach says to you, "You've already played some big games this season, we'd like this other chap to start instead of you." How would you have taken it?' There was nothing they could say to that.

Some readers might be thinking, *He's a lawyer and a referee, he must be some cut-throat bastard*, but that isn't the case at all. I've always wanted to do well, but never at the expense of anyone else. And when I'm refereeing or running touch, I want everyone else to do well because that makes my job easier and means no one is slagging off refereeing standards. I just expected professional rugby to be a meritocracy.

It's not as if I had all these fantasies about being cheered into Twickenham and shouldered off to a standing ovation. But it would have been nice if they'd recognised all the service I'd given to English rugby down the years and said, 'Are there any particular matches you'd like to do? What stadium would you like to be in for your last one? Just say and we can make it a bit special.' Instead, what tends to happen is what happened to me, which leaves people disillusioned and thinking, *Oh, that's what you think of me, thanks very much . . .*

Further evidence that the authorities don't have referees' backs, and seem to be making stuff up as they go along, was the incident between Johnny Sexton and Jaco Peyper after the 2023 Champions Cup final, which La Rochelle won against Leinster

Leinster's Sexton, who didn't play because he was injured, walked on to the pitch and abused Jaco and his touch judges, Karl Dickson and Christophe Ridley. You could clearly see him letting rip as Jaco was on the podium receiving his medal, and you didn't need to be a lip reader to know that was he was saying wasn't very pleasant, to put it mildly.

You might think that Jaco should have reported Sexton, but rarely will a ref do anything if a coach or player swears at them as they're leaving the pitch, or when they're back in the changing room, because they don't want to become a headline. Jaco wanted to avoid being 'the man who got Sexton banned from the World Cup', just as I was 'the man who got Dylan Hartley banned from a Lions tour' (don't worry, there's more on that later).

Referees are also worried they'll be labelled trouble-makers (referees need to build relationships with coaches and players, and they're not going to like you very much if you tell on them, even if what you tell is true). And they're worried they'll be overlooked for any future games involving that team (Sexton's Ireland were one of the favourites for the 2023 World Cup).

So when asked, Jaco and his team said they didn't hear anything. European Rugby didn't believe them, but Jaco and his team weren't prepared to put their names to any statements because they weren't confident that European Rugby would protect them.

European Rugby promised them their names wouldn't be mentioned and said it would write a statement on their behalf (you'd be ripped apart in the criminal justice system for doing that), but when the time came to prosecute Sexton, their names and quotes were all over the transcripts of the judgement. (For the record, Sexton got a three-match ban, making him available for Ireland's opening World Cup game.) As you can imagine, Jaco and his team felt let down, and I don't blame them.

Cricket has it right. If a batter is given out caught behind or lbw and stands their ground or gives the umpire a piece of their mind, they'll be docked a percentage of their match fee. It's not down to the umpire filing a report, it's down to a panel of referees. But in rugby, it's a case of, 'Well, do you want to make a report or not?' To which the answer is usually, 'Of course I don't!'

It reminds me of a nice quote from Howard Webb, who was in charge of hundreds of domestic, European and international games and is now the head of English football referees: 'For a long time, referees have taken a conciliatory approach,' says Howard. 'I did it as well. I didn't want to overreact and ruin the game in the moment. But that's not fared well in the bigger picture, and we need to collectively look at ways we change the trend.'

Referees in all sports lean towards being conciliatory because they don't want to be seen as the bad guy who spoiled a big occasion. That's why referees need people above them to take some decisions out of their hands, to say, 'We don't need to ask the referee, we've got video evidence, we heard what you said on the mic. We suspect you brought the game into disrepute, so we're going to ask you to explain yourself. And if you can't, we're going to charge you.'

If governing bodies stuck up for us, there would be no real need for a referees' union. But rugby's governing bodies don't, which is why we've founded an association of International Rugby Match Officials (IRMO), more of which later.

It's sad that we've had to take that course of action, but we needed to start standing up for ourselves. And by standing up for ourselves, we'll be standing up for referees at all levels, because if people are allowed to get away with abusing refs in professional rugby, you'll see more and more abuse in grassroots rugby, the kind of stuff that's been happening in grassroots football for years.

9

Fallout

My relationship with the IRB's referee selectors didn't improve much in the few years after the 2007 World Cup. Had I not been so young – I was only twenty-eight in 2007 – it might have been the end of me, rugby-wise. And I did think about slipping away from rugby and concentrating on law. As it was, I decided to stick with it, and there were a rocky few years ahead of me.

I was given one game in the 2008 Six Nations but wasn't scheduled to ref another international until the autumn. I said to the selectors, 'You've asked me to go out and prove I've got better, but how can I do that if I haven't got a game for six months?' So they put me in charge of Nelson Mandela's ninetieth birthday game between South Africa and Argentina at Ellis Park in Johannesburg.

That's a great example of the capricious nature of referee selection, because it was the world champions versus third in the world in front of 62,000 of the most passionate rugby fans on the planet. I was really excited to meet Madiba, but he was poorly and didn't make an appearance. And it wasn't exactly a nailbiter, because the Boks hammered the Pumas 63–9.

I was also dropped for using players' first names in 2009, but I thought I was refereeing better than ever before the 2011 World Cup. I refereed a cracking Bledisloe Cup game between Australia and New Zealand in Brisbane a few weeks before it kicked off; I refereed it well, and honestly thought I'd be refereeing the knockout stages again.

But the 2011 World Cup was a horrible experience, and I should have seen it coming. In 2009, I was sent to run touch for a Tri Nations game between the All Blacks and South Africa in Hamilton, and I decided to ref some provincial and school games while I was there. I suppose I was trying to show I was human, but there was still a lot of ill-will towards me. The provincial players were fine, and the schools were really appreciative that an international referee from England was officiating at their games. But I still took quite a bit of flak from fans, and the press was still peddling the line that I was the devil.

Over the years, I've made lots of good Kiwi friends, but rugby is just such a big part of their culture that almost everyone has an opinion on it. So when I returned in 2011, people were telling me to 'fuck off home' while I was warming up. Not exactly rapier wit. People would also stop me in the street or approach me when I was just trying to have a quiet beer in a bar. They'd say, 'What are you doing in our fucking country, mate?' And I'd reply, 'Trying to earn a living, if I'm being honest.'

I refereed four group games at the World Cup, and the Kiwi press got stuck into me early. In the Wales–South Africa game, which was one of the biggest clashes of the group stage, Welsh full-back James Hook kicked a penalty that sailed right over the top of a post. Replays suggested it may have drifted in enough, but one of my touch judges said it had gone wide, so I had to disallow it. The ball took a long time to come back, and I eventually had to ask a ball boy for a new one by signalling the shape of a ball.

The following day, the New Zealand press hammered me. They said the ball had clearly gone between the posts, that I had signalled for the TMO (the TV shape that we signal is quite different to the shape I was signalling to the ball boy) and then changed my mind. Both of those accusations were incorrect, but anyone reading those reports who hadn't seen the game would have concluded I'd had an absolute shocker.

After Wales's 66–0 drubbing of Fiji, they made a big song and dance about me missing a forward pass in the lead-up to one of the Welsh tries. It probably was a forward pass, but it was a breakaway try, and I was about fifty metres behind, and who cared anyway?

I thought I'd done pretty well in my group games, but I was cut for the knockout stages, with no explanation. The day after the final, I did eventually manage to track down Paddy O'Brien, the referee manager for the 2011 RWC, who barely left his room for the whole tournament because he was under so much pressure (he was a Kiwi, it was being played in New Zealand, and they hadn't won the World Cup since the first one in 1987). He couldn't give me a reason I could fully understand.

That whole tournament was badly managed by the selectors. There was no feedback after games, and there were no regular meetings: they just let the officials sink or swim. I felt particularly hard done by, and I mostly sank.

A decision had clearly been made to keep me well away from the All Blacks, because I didn't even run touch for any of their games. And while I was drowning my sorrows in the darkest, dingiest bars of Auckland – all the better not to be spotted in – no one from the IRB thought to ask how I was coping.

By the time Polly turned up, I wasn't in the best shape, physically or mentally. I hadn't done any exercise for two weeks, all I'd done was drink, so I was about 9 kg heavier than when I arrived. We hired one of those massive camper vans and took a whistlestop tour of the North Island, and I got dog's abuse everywhere we went. One day, Polly and I were walking down to Cathedral Cove, which is a beautiful and very hard-to-get-to marine reserve. Suddenly we heard, 'Hey, Barnesy! I still haven't forgiven you for fucking us over in '07!' I was thinking, *What the hell is wrong with this country?*

I was just beginning to relax when I got a call out of the blue telling me I was in charge of the third/fourth-place play-off between Australia and Wales. They must have run out of refs and said, 'We may as well give Barnesy one.'

We returned to Auckland the night before the game, and preparation consisted of a quick chat with my two assistant refs on the Friday morning. Thankfully, the game at Eden Park went off without any hitches, as third/fourth-place play-offs tend to.

After the game, Polly and I ended up in the same nightclub as the Welsh team. Welsh scrum-half Mike Phillips was at the bar, and he jokingly turned to me and said, 'Barnesy, you tosser, want a drink?' while doing the wanker sign. 'Yes, thank you,' I replied, before Polly came tearing up behind me, lunged at Mike and started taking swings at him, while screaming, 'How dare you speak to my partner like that!' In Polly's defence, she'd only heard the tosser part. And she was very aware that I was in a sensitive state, and therefore in full protective mode.

Ryan Jones's method of diffusing the situation was to pick up Polly and deposit her on the other side of the room. Polly's heavily into her karate, so she might even have won that one. I was just relieved there was no one taking photos. Imagine the headline: PHILLIPS ATTACKED BY REFEREE'S PARTNER.

Polly and I attended the final between New Zealand and France, which was an eerie occasion. The All Blacks scored an early try, but then had to bring on their fourth-choice fly-half, Stephen Donald. After that, things got very tight, and the fear in the stadium was palpable. They hadn't won the World Cup since 1987, and now it looked like they were going to slip up again.

I was sitting next to French referee Romain Poite, who was in hysterics the whole game because he was convinced France were going to win, despite being pretty average for most of the tournament. Of course, despite the heroics of French captain Thierry Dusautoir, who scored a try, made a ludicrous number of tackles and won the man-of-the-match award, the All Blacks hung on to win 8–7. Thank God they did, because there would have been months of mourning had they lost.

Not that the All Blacks' triumph stopped the Kiwi press from having another pop at me. One paper reported that Polly was cheering on the French (she was, not because she was anti-Kiwi, but because she wanted the northern hemisphere team, and the underdogs, to win), which they claimed was evidence that I 'still' had a problem with New Zealand.

The big mistake I made after 2007 was choosing not to engage with the media. It felt like the rational thing to do, because it was the media who had whipped the forward pass into such a big deal. But it was mainly the Kiwi media (the UK media didn't really care, probably because my mistake led to a northern hemisphere side beating the southern hemisphere favourites), so imposing a blanket ban didn't make much sense.

I didn't speak to a journalist for three years, and it did further damage to my image. Like everyone else, referee selectors are influenced by the media. So if a referee cultivates a personable media image by doing the occasional interview or podcast or spot of punditry, that's going to help their career.

Not many sporting officials down the years have become celebrities – cricket umpire Dickie Bird springs to mind – but those that do break through serve an important purpose, in that they humanise and demystify their jobs.

The only other celebrity sporting official I can think of is Nigel Owens. He made sure he was in the media a lot, whether it was writing articles or appearing on *Scrum V* in Wales, and that earned him greater respect from the selectors, and also from the fans and players he refereed.

I've no doubt that players sometimes thought, *Nigel's got that wrong, but I'm not going to say anything, because everybody loves him.* I know for a fact that certain commentators were reluctant to criticise him because they told me that when they'd done it before, it had led to a load of social media abuse.

But while Nige was building his profile, I was cultivating an image as a bit of a mummy's boy who likes the sound of his own voice and is too uppity to speak to the media. Once your image is cemented, it's hard to overhaul it. And that media blackout partly explains why people still think I'm this posh rugger bloke from somewhere in the Home Counties.

I'm told the British media was largely fair to me during my career, but I was very disciplined in not reading anything, because very rarely is someone going to say something positive about you. The *Telegraph's* Steve James once gave me man of the match after a game between Northampton and Gloucester. It poured down and the score was something like 8–5, but I refereed it so that they could still have a half-decent game, rather than a complete shit fight (I should probably point out that Steve played for Lydney RFC, where I used to live, and one of the best men at his wedding was a neighbour of mine).

I certainly didn't read any of the papers when I refereed in South Africa or New Zealand, because any games they play get blanket coverage in the lead-up, which will always include a profile of the referee. And if I got slammed in the match reports, I wouldn't have to read them anyway, because my mates would take photos and send them to me. The bastards.

But after the 2011 World Cup, I had a chat with the RFU's head of comms and asked if I was pursuing the right strategy, to which the answer was a resounding no. They wanted to promote refereeing as a career and convinced me that I had a certain responsibility to explain the difficulty of my role and why it wasn't as bad as it was cracked up to be. They also drummed it into me that if I stayed silent, other people would fill the void with untruths.

The media plays a massive part in the game and can make or break a referee. Journalists and pundits essentially decide if you're good or not, and not only are people on social media influenced by them, they're influenced by people on social media. So if a referee makes a big mistake, it can be like getting sucked into a maelstrom from which it feels impossible to escape.

When I spoke at the Rugby Union Writers' Club dinner in 2022, I noted that there was a big difference between writing 'Wayne Barnes got decisions wrong today and had a poor game' and 'Wayne Barnes had an absolute shocker and should never referee a test match again'. The former is measured, the latter is personal and can have negative effects on a referee's mental wellbeing and career prospects.

I've always had a good relationship with former England fly-half Andy Goode – there's some nice footage of me and him having a laugh and a joke towards the end of his career up at Newcastle – but since he retired and moved into punditry, he hasn't stopped berating referees. And not just 'the ref got it wrong', but also personal attacks. If that's the sort of pundit you want to be, fine. But when I saw Andy walking out with the trophy before the European Champions Cup final, as happened this year, I thought, *What does it say about our game that someone who's always bashing refs is a competition ambassador?*

What I find most bizarre is the public criticism from fellow referees. Jonathan Kaplan had a column in the *Telegraph* and set up a website called 'Rate The Ref' (Jonathan hated being criticised, yet there he was slagging off other referees every week). Then there's former international referee Owen Doyle, who writes for the *Irish Times* and whose criticism can be quite spiky.

In 2015, I started working with the head of comms at the RFU, a fantastic woman called Joanna Manning-Cooper, who is now head of comms at the FA. She put together a strategy for me, which definitely helped. If you're popular in the press, and you're liked by the commentators, it can make a big difference because they dictate the narrative. I never became as popular as Nige – I'm not sure I became popular at all – but maybe I became more difficult to dislike.

10

Holding Court

I worry about some of the younger referees nowadays, because they don't have anything to fall back on if the refereeing doesn't work out.

The fact I had another job certainly helped when things weren't going to plan with my refereeing. I knew that if the selectors decided never to pick me again, which was always a possibility, I'd be welcome at 3 Temple Gardens.

My work as a barrister was a release from rugby, and it provided me with perspective. Advocating for clients in court is serious stuff, certainly far more serious than thirty people running around a field with a ball. If I didn't get my preparation right as a barrister, someone might lose their liberty.

Tony Spreadbury's day job was a paramedic, and when you've been scraping people off the floor all week, or you've just had to tell someone their partner is never coming home, refereeing a rugby match is going to feel quite trivial in comparison. Before a game, Spreaders would sometimes say, 'This isn't life and death, I've just come from life and death.'

Spreaders was able to get people to do things through sheer force of energy and enthusiasm, and humour was one of his main attributes as a ref. He was the only ref I knew who commentated on himself during a game, as in, 'Don't worry, lads, Spreaders has seen it.' That scared the shit out of some players because they assumed he was a bit bonkers.

Spreaders also used his humour to defuse situations, although that didn't work with everyone. Some coaches found him quite frustrating, because instead of giving a straight answer to a question, he'd try to deflect it with a joke.

I'm a lawyer, so think in a more analytical way than Spreaders, and was probably stronger in terms of knowing the laws and regulations, but that's maybe why we worked so well together when he was my coach. Spreaders would say to me, 'You can soften the way you speak to players in this situation, and you don't need to go as hard on players in that situation.'

Spreaders taught me not to be triggered by a player's angry, knee-jerk reaction, and that someone shouting in your face immediately after an incident is very different to someone still shouting at you after an incident has been decided on with the help of the TMO.

— ⋆ —

One thing you need to have as a referee is the ability to interact with people: know when to smile and when not to, when to turn a deaf ear, when to turn your back. Like I said earlier, I don't like confrontation – away from work I'm laid-back and like everyone just to get along – but on a rugby field, I was the bloke who ruined everyone's afternoon by making a couple of mistakes, or caused someone to miss a major final by showing them a red card, and that meant having to stand up to lots of angry and upset people over the years.

I'm not sure you can learn all that just from being a referee, it's the kind of stuff you pick up from other areas of your life. And in my case, my legal advocacy has made me a more rounded, emotionally intelligent person.

As a young barrister, I'd meet a client for the first time in the cells of HMP Wormwood Scrubs or HMP Belmarsh. I'd knock on the cell door and say, 'I'm Wayne Barnes and I'm looking after you. Tell me everything we need to know about your case.' They would often be very stressed and wary, and I'd have to be able to build a relationship very quickly, which meant getting my points across succinctly and listening well. I would obviously have to know the laws relating to whatever the alleged offence was, so that they trusted that I knew what I was doing (pulling out a law guide and flicking through it for ten minutes wouldn't have been a good look). The process was very similar to meeting players and coaches in the changing room before a game of rugby.

There is also a lot of crossover between refereeing a game of rugby and courtroom advocacy. I'll never forget the first time I stood up in crown court with my robes on, just as I'll never forget the first time I ran out in my official Premiership refereeing kit. They were both very special moments.

People sometimes ask if wearing a gown and wig in court made me feel powerful, but it made me feel sombre. And it wasn't just me it had that effect on. Suddenly, hardened criminals, people who had done terrible things, would behave with civility and respect. I can't say my refereeing kit inspired such composure in everyone, but it seemed to work for some people.

People don't want long-winded speeches in a courtroom, they want brevity and crispness, because they have short attention spans. But you still have to put on a bit of a performance – slip on a mask and play a role, much like an actor – so that the twelve jurors hang on your every word. And while I preferred to stay under the radar on a rugby field, sometimes I'd be forced on to the stage.

When I was up on the big screen, deliberating over a decision, that was me in advocacy mode, except wearing a different mask, explaining things as simply as possible, so that everyone watching understood. But I'd want to get off that screen as quickly as possible, because I knew it was boring people and it went against my mantra of momentum, momentum, momentum.

You're never completely in control as a barrister, just as you're never completely in control as a referee. But while you have more unpredictable moments as a referee – there are thirty players on the pitch, all doing their own thing – the unpredictable moments in a courtroom will be far more important.

A client might say something unexpected, a juror might fall asleep, or the judge might be a cantankerous-so-and-so and pick you up on something that throws you. In that situation, you have to weigh up, very quickly, whether to thank the judge or plough on, in the hope that the jury didn't hear it. Whatever decision you make, it might alter the outcome of the case.

I didn't just practise advocacy myself, I watched other people doing it as well. And every barrister relates to a jury in their own unique way. One of the tricks I learned from my pupil masters was to talk more quietly during the jury speech, which is the last opportunity a barrister has to put their case across (and which is a staple of courtroom dramas). If you do that, the jury will naturally lean in and hopefully pay that little bit more attention. Although when I tried that before a game at Sale, because I wanted the front rows to pay attention, Sharks head coach Steve Diamond got quite cross and shouted, 'How dare you come into my changing room and talk softly!' I didn't know how to respond to that.

But perhaps the most valuable thing my legal work taught me was the importance of thorough preparation. As a criminal barrister, you get what you're given, whether it's to do with sex, violence, drugs, fraud, whatever. And even if I suspected someone was guilty, I had the responsibility to defend them to the best of my ability.

When I was a junior barrister, a trial might come in at 4 p.m. on Monday and I'd be representing that client at 9 a.m. the following morning. I'd be expected to know that case inside out, so I spent many long nights poring over files and files of paper with a mug of coffee on the go, just as I spent many long nights examining the scrummaging techniques of props.

I'd be lying, however, if I said working in law and being a ref complemented each other perfectly. When I became a partner in a law firm, I'd be about to sit down for dinner with my team the night before a game and I'd get a call saying that one of our corporate clients needed to speak to me because a big issue had blown up in some part of Africa I'd never heard of.

While the boys were having dinner and a couple of drinks, I'd be on a call in my hotel room, trying to set up an internal investigation. Twelve hours later, I'd be refereeing Sharks v. Munster in the Champions Cup.

And back in 2005, when I was still a junior barrister, things got tricky when I was doing a dishonesty case in a magistrates' court in north London.

The vast majority of magistrates' court cases last for a day, and if they do spill into a second, it's almost never the following one, because the magistrates, who have other jobs, have something else on. That's what happened in this case: the trial didn't finish, and the only date everyone was available to reconvene was in nine or ten weeks' time. The problem being, I didn't have my diary with me, so I had to tell them I might need to come back the following week to change things around.

The following day, I found out I couldn't do the new date, not because I had another court case, but because I was refereeing Scotland's game against the Barbarians in Aberdeen. This was only a couple of years into my rugby career and would have been my first taste of the international game, so I simply couldn't drop out.

But when I returned to the court the following week and told them I wouldn't be able to do the new date because I had a clash, they told me they weren't prepared to rearrange it. I said to them, 'Well, I'm not going to be here.' And they replied, 'Mr Barnes, you'll be here . . .'

I chose the rugby over the court case and sent one of my colleagues to look after things while I was up in Aberdeen. I gave her my notes and what I thought was a thorough briefing, but when she turned up to court and explained that it might be tricky cross-examining someone on what they said when she wasn't even present, they adjourned the case.

We got the trial done eventually, and I got my guy acquitted, but afterwards the magistrates asked me to explain why I'd missed the previous date. It was like being back in the headmaster's office. When I told them I'd been refereeing Scotland v. Barbarians in Aberdeen, they weren't impressed and decided to give me a wasted cost order, which meant I had to pay the costs of everyone who did turn up. Anything over £250 would have meant being reported to our regulatory body, what is now the Bar Standards Board. Fortunately, they fined me £249.

Even so, it was a big slap on the wrist, and £249 was quite a lot of money for a junior barrister earning £80 per trial.

People assume barristers make a packet, but if I was doing 'mentions', which are preparatory hearings for big trials, I'd spend a few hours reading up on the case, travel to the court the following morning, sit around waiting for the judge to call the case, and maybe get back to chambers for lunchtime. My reward: £46.50, and I had to pay for my travel.

In case you were wondering, I didn't get paid for Scotland–Barbarians either, because it didn't count as a proper Test match.

11

Back in the Good Books

Luckily, at least for me, the IRB appointed a new referee manager in the summer of 2012, Frenchman Joël Jutge. Joël assured me he thought I was a decent ref and that he would give me an opportunity to prove myself, and I refereed Ireland v. South Africa and Wales v. Australia that autumn.

With Joël's appointment, it felt like a hangover had lifted and I could finally move on from that bloody 2007 World Cup quarter-final.

In 2013, I was even appointed referee for New Zealand v. France in Auckland, and I got on well with their new head coach Steve Hansen. After that game, Steve and I chatted about refereeing at the post-match dinner. His team had won, but he explained that by encouraging the defence to over-compete, I'd made my job more difficult. Why, he asked, hadn't I set the parameters of what was and wasn't acceptable earlier?

That's what I call constructive criticism, from a man who genuinely wanted to improve the game. He thought that if I got better as a referee, rugby would benefit. I appreciated that, and it changed the way I refereed in future.

I was picked for my third World Cup in 2015, which was a bleak experience for the England team and fans, what with the hosts getting knocked out in the group stage, but an amazing tournament for me.

I had spent the previous decade as an international referee being royally entertained everywhere I'd been in the world, especially in the southern hemisphere, where they're particularly proud of their countries. Down there, sponsors want to show off their vineyards and people want to take you out for dinner, or to their game lodge or boat club, or for a walk in the mountains, and while I loved those times, I felt a little embarrassed because we didn't reciprocate when their referees came to England. They'd turn up, get dropped off at the Lensbury Club in Teddington and be left to their own devices. But the 2015 World Cup was my chance to give back and show off my country.

I'd arranged with the Royal Marines for us to train with them at the Commando Training Centre in Lympstone, Devon, which was great for some of the young, aspiring assistant referees, not so much for the video referees. Graham Hughes, who was in his mid-fifties, probably hadn't seen a gym for about two decades.

During the day, the Marines had us scrambling across commando nets, swinging across monkey bars and ropes, diving through water tunnels, driving power boats and shooting each other with water cannons. And in the evening, we listened to some great talks from ex and current Marines. I'm sure not everybody loved every minute of it, but it brought us all together quite nicely.

I also helped arrange a welcoming ceremony for the match officials in Westminster Abbey, with speeches from World Rugby chairman Bernard Lapasset and Tony Spreadbury. I hoped my fellow officials were eating, drinking, laughing and taking in the sumptuous surroundings while thinking, *This makes me feel special, like I'm an integral part of this tournament.*

There were also events throughout the tournament, including dinner at Lincoln's Inn with many leading barristers, a day in the Houses of Parliament and a walk down Downing Street, which the public aren't allowed to do any more.

There happened to be a cabinet meeting taking place, so we stood and watched all these ministers going in and out of Number 10. The strength-and-conditioning coach had his kids with him, and one of them broke ranks and knocked on the door, thinking he'd be let in, at which point we were surrounded by police. Luckily, none of us got tasered.

One evening, we witnessed the Ceremony of the Keys, which is when the Yeomen Warders, better known as the Beefeaters, lock up the Tower of London for the night which has been happening since the fourteenth century. Afterwards, we repaired to the Beefeaters' very own pub, which is in the middle of the Tower, and had a few beers and a raffle, which was a bit tricky to explain to the French officials. But what a special evening, and I'm sure everybody else thought the same.

I had a room at the spectacular Landmark Hotel in Marylebone (God knows how much that cost the organisers), but our daughter was about twelve months old and Polly was back at work full time, so I probably only stayed there four or five times in eight weeks. (I should have sublet it: I would have made enough to retire on.) That meant I missed out on some fun nights, but the bonds had already been forged.

One night I wasn't going to miss out on was the traditional pre-knockout-stage celebration, which took place on the Monday before the weekend's quarter-finals. Former Saracens fly-half Glen Jackson was one of the refs and he took us all to this great Italian restaurant with a cellar. That was the perfect venue, because people didn't need to see a load of World Cup officials getting hammered in the middle of the tournament.

That wasn't the first time my wig and gown had been used in a kangaroo courtroom, although it was probably the last. Nigel Owens, who was inevitably the judge, paired the wig and gown with a pair of Superman boxer shorts. And nothing else. Romain Poite was the enforcer of the fines, and he got into character by dressing up in his military combats (he used to be a copper). I was the prosecutor, presenting the cases, and there were also lads dressed as the Seven Dwarfs (I can't remember why).

Our strength-and-conditioning coach ended up doing commando rolls across tables (blame the Marines), we had ex-Munster players dressed in Leinster kit, and a very entertaining night was had by all. The following morning, I discovered that the strength-and-conditioning coach had got so pissed that he spent five minutes banging on the window of Madame Tussauds because he thought Kylie Minogue was trying to beckon him in.

I refereed the quarter-final between South Africa v. Wales at Twickenham, which was a surreal and memorable day. Because I live in Twickenham, we had our team meeting in my kitchen, over a spot of lunch, before walking to the stadium. That was the first time I'd walked to a Rugby World Cup match, and it was a great experience. Welsh and South Africans were mingling without any trouble, and I was able to really savour the atmosphere.

Wales were leading with five minutes to go, before Duane Vermeulen broke off the back of a scrum and offloaded to Fourie du Preez, who went over in the corner. That evening, we headed to a local boozer that former England lock Simon Shaw part-owned, and there must have been five hundred people in there, mostly Welsh and South African fans, but also Aussie commentary teams because the Wallabies were playing Scotland at Twickenham the next day. (When I told football referee Howard Webb that story, he looked at me like I was mad and said, 'We jump straight in a car after a game and head home.')

My team and I went through the same pre-match routine for the semi-final between Australia and Argentina: all of us sat around my kitchen table, having a bite to eat and chatting about what to expect from the game, before swinging our bags over our shoulders and heading to Twickenham.

Even when England were bundled out of the tournament early, I still expected Nigel Owens rather than me to referee the final. That's almost always how it works: at my first World Cup in 2007, Alain Rolland was favourite to referee the big one, and he did, and it was the same with Craig Joubert in 2011. But Wales had a chance of reaching the final in 2015 (which would have ruled out Nige) and I knew that, if I was refereeing well, I'd be in with a shout.

As it turned out, I did referee well, but when Wales were beaten by South Africa in the quarter-finals, Nige became nailed on for the job, and I was appointed as an assistant referee. And I had no problem with that, because Nige was one hell of a referee, and a great friend too.

Nige and I had the same basic philosophy, which was wanting every game we refereed to flow. However, we differed in how we made that happen. Nige allowed more things to go and was more likely to talk players out of things. For example, if someone was on the wrong side, he'd tell them to get out of the way, rather than go straight for his whistle. My way was to set standards early on, which meant a bit more whistling, in the hope that both teams would try to stay on the right side of the law for the rest of the game.

Nige would be the first to admit that he wasn't one of those refs who knew the law book back to front, but he made that a virtue. His attitude was, 'Do I really need to be blowing my whistle for that kind of stuff? I don't think so.'

Players trusted Nige simply because he was a decent bloke. It's just human nature that if you're a bit of an arsehole, players aren't going to like you, which means they're less likely to do what you tell them. But if you're engaging and have a sense of humour, they are more likely to fall into line.

Familiarity was one of Nige's trump cards. When Nige was out in the middle, players felt comforted. He had a nice avuncular way about him, which meant he was able to make people smile even when he didn't mean to.

That ability to tickle people as a referee is very rare and extremely valuable in elite rugby, and Nige has got a long list of classic one-liners, the best of which was probably, 'I'm straighter than that one,' delivered deadpan to Harlequins hooker Dave Ward after a crooked throw. Not only does that kind of stuff endear you to players, but it also endears you to commentators, journalists and fans.

Nige led the way in humanising rugby referees, in that people saw him as a person and not just that bloke who was trying to spoil everyone's fun. In turn, that helped us as a group. It was Nige who made me realise that not speaking to the media after the 2007 World Cup was doing none of us any favours, because I was demonising our role, making us seem aloof and arrogant.

Sometimes Nige would get the balance slightly wrong and say something during a game that commentators, journalists and fans found funny, but which irritated the players. One incident that comes to mind was when he called England captain Chris Robshaw 'Christopher' at the end of a game between England and France. England had just lost the Six Nations Championship in the final seconds and Robshaw was obviously pissed off, and now he had the referee talking to him like a teacher to a naughty schoolboy.

I know the England team were a bit annoyed about that, but it soon blew over because it was 'just Nige', the mischievous Welshman, the like of whom rugby union will never see again. Imagine if I'd ever called Johnny Sexton 'Jonathan'! I'd be portrayed as a stereotypically haughty English twat.

Nige and I have been through so much together since those early days on the sevens circuit. He was there for me in 2007 when I was copping it from all directions, and we were there for each other in 2011, when both of us were going through a rough time, albeit for different reasons.

We're still close now and like to tease each other about the old days. I sometimes remind Nigel that when he announced that he was gay, I got more calls from friends than he did because they'd just read the headline: 'Rugby referee comes out.' And Nigel still blames me for missing a forward pass in the 2015 World Cup final. He'll say to me, 'You didn't know what a forward pass was then and you still haven't learned.'

I wasn't overly keen on going to the 2019 World Cup in Japan. It meant being away from home, and not seeing

Polly or the kids, for ten weeks. And while I'd spent a bit of time in Japan before, and enjoyed it, I wondered if the unfamiliarity, from the language to the food, would make it a bit of a grind.

Before the tournament started, we had a team-building camp. And it was a shambles. After two days, we'd barely spoken about rugby, even though there was some big stuff that needed discussing, particularly to do with the new high-tackle framework.

We were going straight from the camp to a meeting with the coaches, and I was getting really worried that I wouldn't be able to tell them what a yellow- or red-card situation was going to look like. So on our last night, a few of us took the management aside and said, 'Look, everyone is getting a little bit nervous, can you explain what's expected of us?' The whole situation was just odd.

We stayed in an amazing place next to Tokyo Station, bang in the middle of the city, but things had been badly planned. Our training pitch was an hour's drive away, so we just didn't go there. Instead, we found patches of grass to train on (Tokyo isn't the greenest city in the world) or ran up hills.

Inevitably, the first weekend of games was a bit all over the place, because the refs didn't have clarity. Then came the public rebuke from World Rugby, which I've expanded on elsewhere in these pages. But a siege mentality kicked in after that; we became tighter as a group and performed well. In fact, I can't remember a World Cup with fewer refereeing controversies.

After the group stage, I got to see parts of Japan I'd never seen before. The people were so welcoming and very keen to show off their country, and I suddenly realised what an amazing place Japan is. I was wined and dined in Osaka and Fukuoka, shown shrines and even taken out to the rainforest. As for local fans, they were spectacular. Even Typhoon Hagibis, which caused the cancellation of three group games, added to the sense of excitement, although of course it caused a lot of devastation and loss of life.

Polly arrived on the morning of the typhoon, on one of the last planes to land before the airport was shut. None of the buses or trains out of the airport were running, but she managed to cadge a lift with someone from the RFU. Polly had planned to watch New Zealand v. Italy in Toyota, which I was meant to be involved in, but that was one of the games that was called off. We'd then planned to watch Scotland v. Japan in Yokohama together, but I was one of a group of refs shipped off to Osaka. We told ourselves they were protecting refereeing royalty, like during a war, but they'd actually just moved our games. Meanwhile, poor Polly was locked in my hotel with the rest of the officials.

After the quarter-finals, I was told I wouldn't be reffing either of the semis, but that if England didn't make the final – which most people expected to happen because they were up against the All Blacks – I'd be in charge. Of course, England played brilliantly and knocked the All Blacks out, but I didn't mope, even though it also meant that Polly wouldn't be coming back out to see me. I went along to the final in Yokohama and cheered England on, because I was an England fan, I knew all the players and I wanted them to do well.

12

Cheatgate

My first Premiership final was Wasps v. Leicester in 2008, which happened to be Lawrence Dallaglio's last game before slipping into retirement.

Wasps had a load of players at the 2007 World Cup and were tenth at Christmas, before finishing like a train to make the play-offs. During the build-up, Leicester made some noise in the press about targeting the Wasps scrum, but Wasps were leading 26–6 at half-time and seemed to be nailed on for the win.

Leicester had just scored their first try and narrowed the lead to fifteen points when Wasps lost their second starting prop to injury, which meant we had to revert to uncontested scrums (both sides only had to have one prop on the bench back in 2008). That's when Tigers skipper Martin Corry said to me, 'Come on, they're obviously going uncontested because they know they've got a weaker scrum.' I replied, 'They've actually won two scrum penalties to none so far.'

Dallaglio was substituted on sixty-seven minutes, and I thought he needed to be given a proper send-off because he's a genuine icon of the English game. So when I saw his number was up, I grabbed the ball and stopped the game so that the 81,000 fans at Twickenham could give him a standing ovation. After all, he would have been a hero to the Leicester fans as well, having been an integral part of the England team that won the World Cup in 2003 (for the record, Wasps went on to win 26–16).

I thought about that moment when I was refereeing my last ever regular-season game between Bristol and Gloucester in May 2023. There were a couple of Bristol legends playing their last games for the club that day, Tonga's Charles Piutau and Fiji's Semi Radradra, and they were allowed to just slip away without any fanfare, which I thought was a shame.

Prior to the 2013 Premiership final between Leicester and Northampton, both sides' staff had a reputation for hot-headedness – and in particular Leicester head coach Richard Cockerill was always so angry when I was around and seemed to genuinely despise me. I'd always had a good relationship with the players, though, but the moment I walked into Saints' changing room that day, to check boots and pass on final reminders to their captain Dylan Hartley and the rest of their front row, I sensed there was something slightly odd going on. As a lawyer, you need to know what you're getting yourself into, so I'd developed sensitive antennae.

Even before a big game at Twickenham, there's usually some light-hearted banter, but Saints' changing room was like a funeral parlour. That can be a sign of extra focus, but there was a frostiness that made me slightly uneasy.

I'd always got on well with Dylan, just as I did lots of other captains. We'd often chat before and during a game, but this time he was off talking to other people. I knew quite a few Saints players quite well, people like Ben Foden and Tom Wood, because they'd been in the England set-up. But that day, nobody seemed to want to engage and have that 'What can I do for you?' chat I normally had. I even said to my assistant referees afterwards, 'That was a bit different . . .'

The first half was surprisingly open, but it had an edge, as you'd expect for an East Midlands derby.

After twenty-odd minutes, Leicester fly-half Toby Flood had to go off after a crunching tackle from Courtney Lawes. He was replaced by George Ford, and as George was lining up his first kick at goal, Northampton assistant coach Alan Dickens, who I have a lot of time for, ran on with some water and started saying, 'Don't fuckin' bottle it! Don't fuckin' bottle it!' I thought I needed to say to him, 'Hold on, mate. You're the water carrier, he's a 20-year-old player, that's not appropriate.'

Dylan then started chuntering after I penalised his prop Soane Tonga'uiha for slipping his binding.

'As usual, he's against us,' said Dylan, which I can ignore on the odd occasion. But there's only so much a referee can tolerate, because constant chuntering from a captain erodes the trust of the rest of that team's players. And when players lose trust in a referee's ability to make correct decisions, it becomes very tough for that referee to orchestrate proceedings.

When Dylan repeated those words, just before half-time, I took him aside and said to him, 'Look, this isn't how you behave as a captain. Please keep your comments to yourself or I may have to deal with it.' He said he wasn't talking to me, and I replied, 'If I *think* it's to me, I'll have to deal with it. Do you understand?'

Dylan said that was fine and I hoped that was the end of it. Rather than rolling my sleeves up and penalising everything, which referees never want to do, I'd be able to stay out of the way and let the game flow. How naive I was.

With about ten seconds to go in the first half, George Ford missed a long-range penalty and all Saints fly-half Stephen Myler had to do was drop-kick the ball into touch, on the bounce, to bring the half to a close. But despite me telling him, 'You can't kick the ball straight out,' three or four times, he did exactly that. Maybe my Forest of Dean burr made 'can't' sound like 'can'. Whatever Myler heard, he was furious, as were the rest of his team, and it turned into a total shitshow.

I wanted to get off the pitch myself, to gather my thoughts and recalibrate, but now we had to have a scrum. Meanwhile, a load of kids had run on the pitch to do a half-time dance routine. The commentator Nick Mullins even pulled out the line, 'Some people are on the pitch! They think it's all over!' but this situation was considerably less joyous than Wembley 1966.

After the kids had been shooed off, Leicester proceeded to steamroller Saints' scrum and I had no option but to award a penalty, bang in front of the posts. That's when Dylan turned to me and called me a 'fucking cheat'.

I'd been called many things in my career, and I can cope with a bit of bad language. In the changing room before a game, Joe Marler would often greet me with, 'I'll get it out of the way and call you a twat now, to save myself from getting sent off.' I was once told that if a player is smiling when they swear at you, that's acceptable. That's not bad advice, unless that player has psychopathic tendencies. I suppose that's one of the beauties of the English language, that you can say exactly the same thing in two different situations and end up with two completely different outcomes.

If I give a decision a player isn't happy with (or don't give a decision they think I should make), they might respond with 'For fuck's sake', but as long as they don't scream it at me, that's fine. And if a player does scream something at me, I'll usually smile and remind them that I don't scream at them – or that I get people screaming at me at home and I could do without it today.

I've never subscribed to the idea that you shouldn't send someone off early in the game because it ruins the spectacle. If it's a red card, it's a red card, whenever it happens, because if you ignore it other players will be able to say, 'Well, he got away with it, that sort of behaviour is obviously acceptable with this ref.'

But a referee should also consider what's best for the game. That means turning a deaf ear to most stuff players say, because if you showed a card to every player who got annoyed and sweary about a decision, most games would finish with about ten players on the pitch.

There are so many grey areas in rugby, and a referee should be allowed to apply common sense within those grey areas, although the bosses sometimes think differently. In 2016, I refereed a Champions Cup game between Clermont and Ospreys. Seventeen minutes into the game, a ruck formed and I stood where I usually stood, looking at the defensive line, making sure they were onside. Suddenly, Clermont's Georgian flanker Viktor Kolelishvili came flying towards me and gave me a big shove.

First I thought, *Thank God I didn't go over like Paul Alcock when he was pushed by Paolo Di Canio back in the day* (that must have been all the core stability training I do). Then I thought, *Shit, strictly speaking I should send him off here . . .* But instead of sending him off, I decided to say, 'Look, you can't be pushing referees, next time just tell me to get out of the way.'

I thought that was the best decision for the player and the game, because he did shove me in the context of me being in his way, and I didn't want it to become this big thing that blew up into a headline. My bosses disagreed, and Kolelishvili was given a fourteen-week ban, which I thought was way too harsh. Saying that, he was very apologetic the next time I refereed him.

A player saying, 'You're a disgrace,' is different to saying, 'That's a disgraceful decision.' The first is probably a red card, the second is probably a yellow, depending on how in your face they are and how aggressively they say it. But when your integrity is called into question as a referee, it's like someone dropping something heavy on your toe – you have an automatic, visceral reaction.

If you watch the footage of that day, you can see how angry I am, as if I'm thinking, *How fucking dare you.* I even give Dylan a slightly theatrical send-off, thumb over the shoulder, which is slightly embarrassing, but shows how incensed I was.

Showing Dylan that red card was not something I remotely enjoyed doing. No referee wants to ruin a game as a contest and spoil everyone's afternoon, because we all come from rugby backgrounds, whether we're former pros – Glen Jackson, Nic Berry, Karl Dickson, John Lacey – or, like me, have just been steeped in the game since childhood. Like players, we sing a lot, we drink together, we celebrate and commiserate. We love the game!

Suddenly, I was in the limelight, the centre of everything – the first referee to show a red card in a Premiership final. But I really didn't have much of a choice. The authorities talk a lot about the game's values, integrity and respect for officials among them. And had I not shown Dylan that red card, it would have given the green light for players, coaches and fans at every level to abuse referees.

It's not like Dylan appealed my decision. He just looked affronted before trudging off. Plus, none of his teammates jumped to his defence, which was quite telling.

After telling Saints vice-captain Tom Wood what had happened word for word (I wanted to do that while the incident was still fresh in my mind), George Ford slotted the penalty. And as I was walking into the changing room, I thought, *So much for staying under the radar. If only Stephen Myler had listened . . .*

In the changing room at half-time, I realised what had happened was a very big deal. Saints' coaching team were screaming and shouting about it and it dawned on me that I'd just sent off a player who was supposed to be going on a Lions tour a week later. I prided myself on my communication skills, which I'd honed in my day job – explaining myself succinctly and clearly, persuading people to trust me. But Dylan clearly hadn't bought into what I was trying to tell him.

After the game, which Leicester won quite comfortably, I knew every headline would be about that Dylan red card. And therefore me. I'd usually stay on the pitch to get my medal (which I always hated doing, because I never thought the game was about me), but on this occasion I thought, *I'm not hanging around, that would be like chucking fuel onto the flames,* and headed for the tunnel. But as I entered the tunnel, a female dignitary from Northampton Saints came up to me and started shouting, 'I can't believe what you've done!' *What I've done?* I thought, but before I could say anything, one of my touch judges grabbed me and dragged me to the changing room.

If you're a lover of dark comedy, you'll like this next bit. It just so happened that it was my stag do that weekend.

All my mates were in a box in the North Stand, which was a gift from Premiership Rugby, and I had to meet them in there afterwards. I spoke to security and asked if they could smuggle me up there via a back passage, and when I reached the box, there was a sign on the door that read, GUESTS OF WAYNE BARNES. That explained why there were loads of Northampton fans milling around looking angry. When I walked in, a big cheer went up from my mates and one of them shouted, 'Here comes the fucking cheat!' Cue uproarious laughter. *Oh great*, I thought, *this is all I need . . .*

My mates wanted to dress me up in my most garish West Country gear, which I didn't think was a good idea. I said to them, 'I can't be seen in fancy dress, not after what's just happened,' so they stuck a coat over my head, dragged me across the car park and bundled me on to a minibus, like I was some serial killer from the 1970s about to be whisked off to prison.

They then wound masking tape around my head, chest and legs to keep me in my seat, before taping a bottle of White Lightning to each hand and informing me that we were off on a West Country cider tour. My nickname from then on was 'Edward Cider Hands', and I wasn't allowed to stop for a piss until I'd drunk it all. There has been no stranger post-match rehydration routine.

I managed to get a few pints down me that night, but I was quite sad and emotional, and certainly wasn't in celebration mode. I had the disciplinary hearing the following morning (at least that was over the phone, so I could do it from my hotel room) and I couldn't get the sending-off out of my mind.

I sometimes say to fans, 'I never headbutted, punched or screamed and shouted at anyone, yet it's me who gets accused of ruining games?' But that night, I kept saying to my mates, "What if he gets off because of a lack of evidence? I've then wrongly sent off the captain of the losing team in a Premiership final. My credibility will be in tatters.'

People think referees go home after a game and carry on as normal, whatever happened. But if we get decisions wrong and screw up big games, that has consequences for us too. Our personal life is adversely affected, and we run the risk of not getting selected for big games in the future.

I gave evidence to the disciplinary hearing the following day. The chair of the disciplinary committee was the Judge Advocate General of the Armed Forces, Jeff Blackett, an independent lawyer. Dylan also had a lawyer asking me questions on his behalf and it became clear that Northampton's story had changed. Immediately after the game, Northampton told my manager that Dylan's 'fucking cheat' comment was said to opposition hooker Tom Youngs. But at the hearing they said he was saying it *about* Tom Youngs to Northampton prop Soane Tonga'uiha.

Meanwhile, my story hadn't changed at all. When they asked me if I could have made a mistake, I replied, 'If I had any doubt, I wouldn't have sent him off. But I have no doubt.' The panel found Dylan guilty and gave him a lengthy ban, which meant he missed the Lions tour. There have been allegations since that he was stitched up, which I've never understood. The panel heard two sets of evidence and thought mine was more compelling, simple as that.

Fast forward six weeks, and I'm getting married to Polly at Lincoln's Inn chapel on the day of the third Lions Test against Australia. Unfortunately, we messed up the timings, and the wedding ceremony and the match kicked off at exactly the same time. At one point, I looked out at the congregation and there were people openly watching the match on iPhones and iPads. When Tony Spreadbury finished his reading, he turned to the chaplain and said, 'By the way, John, we're 9–3 up in Australia . . .'

We decided on a reception in France, mad as it sounds. We had two Eurostar carriages to ourselves and took a one-man band with us. When we arrived in Paris, we all bundled on to a coach before catching a boat to an island on the Seine, where my friend had an amazing restaurant. We were greeted by a French oompah band, who played almost non-stop for the next eight or nine hours. What a wonderful day that was, never to be forgotten.

After our wedding, Polly and I went off on honeymoon, which included a bit of sea and sun in the Maldives. The island we were on was tiny, with about twenty huts dotted about the place. It felt like we were in the most remote place on earth, which was just perfect.

Then one night, we were sitting on the veranda, sipping cocktails, when a boat pulled into the jetty and a couple jumped off. I thought, *Blimey, that bloke is massive.* A couple of minutes later, I felt a big hand on my shoulder.

And when I turned around, who was standing there but Tom Youngs and his wife Tiff.

Tom, who was on holiday after the victorious Lions tour (he played in all three Tests), said to me, 'Wouldn't this be a lovely photo for Dylan?' And after a quick chat, Tom and Tiff went on their way. That was not a time to talk about rugby. And it certainly wasn't the place for a photo.

Six years later, I was invited to a boozy lunch and found myself sitting next to Dorian West, Northampton's forwards coach from that day. It was the first time we'd discussed 'that game'. He blamed himself for creating such a hostile atmosphere in the Saints camp and therefore how that game panned out. The build-up was all about how everyone was against them, from the authorities to the media. That made sense, because 'he's against us' was exactly what Dylan kept saying before calling me a cheat. Sometimes, that 'us against them' approach works because it gives players an edge. But it's a very fine line between arousal and over-arousal, as any teenage boy will tell you.

I certainly didn't harbour any hard feelings towards Dylan because, while I had to send him off, I still understood that professional sportspeople are ferociously competitive, desperately want to win and will sometimes do and say things they'll regret. Likewise, most players understand that referees have a very difficult job and don't mean to get things wrong.

When Eddie Jones became England head coach, he asked me who the best captains in the league were and I said Dylan was one of them. I acknowledged that there was a big elephant in the room whenever we met, but also that he led his team well, asked questions at the right time, didn't scream and shout and was normally polite. A few weeks later, Dylan was appointed England captain.

Dylan and I have never spoken about that final, but whenever I worked with England over the next few years, we never had a problem. Saying that, the last time we met, at some dinner or other, he introduced me to someone with the words, 'This is the person who almost ruined my career.' That was one of those moments when you chuckle uncomfortably and quickly move on.

I know from my work as a barrister that people can tell a story so often that they eventually believe it, even if all the evidence proves it's not true. I've represented people who were utterly convinced of their innocence despite their DNA being all over the crime scene, and it wouldn't surprise me if Dylan honestly believes he didn't call me a cheat that fateful day at Twickenham.

13

Techno

As you won't be surprised to learn, I've been a big advocate of technology in rugby since refereeing that fateful World Cup quarter-final in 2007. We should be helping referees as much as possible, which means taking them out of the game as much as possible, instead of asking them to make more and more decisions.

I once did a presentation for some football referees, around the time VAR was being introduced, and there was a lot of pushback against it. They thought it undermined their authority, but I said to them, 'At some point, you'll have to make a decision you're not quite sure about that will potentially define your career. Why would you not want to take a second look at it?' If only I'd been able to take a second look at 'that' forward pass in 2007 – it would have taken all of five seconds – the next few years of my life would have been a whole lot easier.

The real problem with VAR hasn't been the technology itself but how it's been implemented. That's the thing about technology, it's only as good as the people at the controls, and it's only as clear as the laws themselves.

In most other sports, the replays take place on big screens, and the refs are mic'd up so you can hear their deliberations. That means everyone watching feels a part of the process, and in sports like cricket, tennis and both codes of rugby, technology has become part of the show. But in football, VAR is like a dirty secret.

Unlike with TMO referrals in rugby, which are almost always immediate, it's common to see players and fans celebrating a goal for ten or fifteen seconds before the referee refers a goal to VAR. Then the referee will scurry off to the side of the pitch and watch the replays on a small screen, before suddenly signalling his or her decision. It doesn't help that some of the laws they're deciding on, such as handball and offside, are very murky.

In any sport, you've got to get the big stuff right, other- wise the whole enterprise is undermined. As long as the technology exists, you can't have an 'oh well, you win some, you lose some' attitude, like when England won the football World Cup in 1966. Back then, the linesman decided Geoff Hurst's shot crossed the line and that was the end of it. Actually, it wasn't, because people haven't stopped talking about it since, but my point is, there simply wasn't the technology to overrule the on-field decision. But if everyone watching on TV can see that the ball has crossed the line, as happened when England played Germany in the 2010 World Cup and Frank Lampard's shot was ruled out even though the ball almost ended up in the back of the net, the sport looks ridiculous.

But what some sports haven't got right at the moment is knowing when to use technology. While I'm a technology advocate, I also think it should be used sparingly. It shouldn't be about trying to get every decision right, it should be about the stuff we all saw on TV and the referee obviously missed.

In South Africa, they've been trialling a chip in the ball, which will tell if a ball has been passed forward. That's a great idea – in theory. My worry is that it won't just be used to pick up forward passes that lead directly to tries, it will be used to pick up every borderline forward pass that happens in a match.

Technology can be open to manipulation, because while the broadcast is run by the organisers at World Cups, during Rugby Championship and Six Nations games, it's run by the home team's own broadcaster, so it's not truly independent. In the 2014 Rugby Championship, I refereed South Africa v. New Zealand in Johannesburg. With a couple of minutes to go, and the All Blacks leading by a point, Schalk Burger was tackled and I thought nothing of it. But it was replayed on the big screen about six times in a minute, and once I'd seen that the tackle on Burger was high, I had to review it.

Pat Lambie kicked the penalty, the Springboks won by two points and New Zealand couldn't really argue because they'd all seen what I'd seen. All Blacks head coach Steve Hansen was really good about it, but it was clear that some countries were using the big screen as a tool to pressure officials.

Hansen was one of the good guys, despite his All Blacks side losing quite a few games I refereed. After the game New Zealand lost to Ireland in Dublin in 2018, he said to me, 'How do you think today went?' I told him I thought it had gone pretty well, and he replied, 'Yep, I'd give you nine out of ten. But my overall win ratio is ninety-one per cent without you and fifty-four per cent with you. Now will you fuck off and retire.'

Using the TMO doesn't always help make a game flow. There was a maddening incident in the autumn international between England and Argentina in 2022: Owen Farrell threw a stray pass under pressure from Pumas prop Thomas Gallo and Santiago Carreras scooped the ball up, ran the length of the field and scored. But the officials spent about two minutes deciding whether or not it had flicked Gallo's fingertips or not before awarding the try. I'm not blaming the officials, they were just doing what they'd been told, but I did wonder why a 'snicko' system, like they have in cricket to judge whether the ball has hit the bat, isn't used in rugby.

Another similar example happened during a game between France and Australia. The TMO asked for a replay of a potential piece of foul play and they couldn't, or wouldn't, find it, so eventually I had to restart the game and explain to the captains that the producers had drawn a blank. Afterwards, Wallabies head coach Michael Cheika, who can be a bit grumpy but was always fair with me, told me I should have waited until they found it. I said to him, 'But we spent two minutes looking for it, how long did you expect?' He replied, 'As long as it took.'

That raised a pertinent point: yes, we want to get decisions right, but how far do you force it? Sometimes you just have to accept that while something untoward might have taken place, we just don't have the right camera angle to confirm it, and we have to keep the game moving.

It's also a case of being careful what you wish for, as VAR offside decisions in football have demonstrated. People spent decades grumbling about dodgy offsides, and when VAR came along, people started complaining about its accuracy because offsides were being given when attackers were literally a toe beyond the line. In rugby, we could put a GPS on every player so that every time a player was offside, even by a centimetre, a hooter would be triggered. But that would add so many more stoppages, and fans don't want stoppages, they want flow.

Sport is, of course, entertainment. That's why TV executives are constantly wanting to improve the spectacle. That means fewer and quicker TMO referrals, which is why World Rugby introduced the 'bunker' for the 2023 World Cup.

Under the new bunker system, the referee will issue a yellow card (having looked at a maximum of two replays, because they want to keep things moving and don't want nasty incidents being shown over and over on the big screen) and officials in a central bunker will review the incident, using all the available technology and footage. Once the ten-minute sinbin period has elapsed, the yellow card is either upheld and the player returns to the field, or it's upgraded to a red card and the player is permanently excluded.

Like VAR in football, it was hoped that the bunker would help speed up the game and get the major decisions right. There was a worry that too many big games were being decided by red cards, so there was a big push from the unions to add a level of scrutiny and security. But while VAR had been trialled for a couple of years before it was introduced at a football World Cup, the bunker was first trialled a few months before the 2023 Rugby World Cup.

That's pretty typical of World Rugby. At the previous World Cup, they trialled the high-tackle sanction framework, which had the noble aim of reducing head injuries. But the referees had no idea how it was supposed to work. Two days before the tournament kicked off, we had to go to World Rugby and say, 'We need to understand what's happening, nobody's thought to tell us.' As it was, there were quite a lot of yellow and red cards at the start of the tournament, before they fell away as referees got to grips with it.

At the 2011 World Cup, it was the tip-tackle that had everyone confused. I was on touch for the semi-final between Wales and France, when Welsh skipper Sam Warburton was sent off after only seventeen minutes for a tip-tackle on Vincent Clerc. The law had been fiddled with for the previous couple of years, and referee Alain Rolland was technically right to show a red card. But there had been three almost identical tip-tackles in the tournament before then, and they'd all resulted in a yellow.

It all happened so quickly that Wales replacement Martyn Williams said to me, 'Barnesy, what's happened?' And I replied, 'I think he's been yellow-carded.' A couple of minutes later, Martyn wandered over to me and said, 'You twat, he sent him off.'

Just before the Lions tour of South Africa in 2009, the IRB suddenly decided to change the ruck law. Previously, if a player made a tackle, they had to rejoin the ruck from their own side, through what is called 'the gate'. But now, a tackler could rejoin the ruck from anywhere. In other words, they could make a tackle, jump straight back up and compete for the ball, even if it was from the direction of the opponents' try line. Not for the first time, the lawmakers hadn't thought through the consequences.

Before the Lions' game against Free State Cheetahs, Cheetahs flanker Heinrich Brüssow, who had played once for the Springboks off the bench but was a relative unknown, sought me out and asked if it would be legal to go straight from the tackle to competing for the ball, even if it was from the direction of the opponents' try line. I told him he could, because the law had changed.

I was nervous about refereeing that game. I'd always been a big Lions fan, and I'd worked with the English players in the team, so I was worried about coming across as biased towards them. That's why they didn't usually appoint British or Irish refs for Lions games! And now I had to deal with this ill-conceived law change. Unsurprisingly, Brüssow, a short barrel of a man, stole a ton of Lions balls, and the tourists, who weren't yet up to speed, only just scraped the win, courtesy of a last-ditch penalty I awarded for holding on.

Lions head coach Ian McGeechan was quite critical of me in his post-match interviews, and the next time I spoke to him, he asked why I was allowing players to steal the ball from an offside position. I had to remind him that the law had changed and Brüssow hadn't done anything wrong. On the back of that performance, Brüssow started for South Africa in the first Test against the Lions and was a real nuisance again in the Springboks' victory.

But this new law looked atrocious and was a nightmare to referee – as usual, us refs hadn't been consulted but ended up having to deal with the shitshow – and four or five years later, the authorities changed the law back so that tacklers had to rejoin a ruck from their own side again.

We were nearly lumbered with a third card at the 2019 World Cup. As now, the authorities were concerned that too many players would be sent off, and about two weeks before the opening game, World Rugby chairman Bill Beaumont phoned to tell me that some of the southern hemisphere unions were touting the idea of an orange card, which a referee would show if a player did something dangerous by accident and would lead to twenty minutes in the sinbin. I said to Bill, 'Look, it might be a great suggestion, but we're two weeks out from the World Cup and it hasn't been trialled.'

On that occasion, World Rugby didn't yield to pressure and the orange card was put on ice. A twenty-minute red card, which allows teams to replace someone who has been sent off after twenty minutes, was also rejected before the 2023 World Cup, despite it being used in Super Rugby. Fans of the twenty-minute red card believe it stops accidental head collisions from spoiling games. However, World Rugby argued that it undermined the game's commitment to reducing the number of concussions.

I liked that the bunker reduced pressure on referees, in that I could literally leave my red card at home, and I'd no longer have to assess an incident of foul play while standing in the middle of the pitch being heckled by 80,000 French people. Plus, as with cricket and tennis when a third umpire or Hawkeye decision flashes up on the screen, everyone accepts it and moves on. And if they don't, because rugby has more grey areas than cricket and tennis, at least they don't blame me!

I thought World Rugby missed a trick by not filling the bunker with ex-coaches and/or players, because they're the ones who always tell us we keep getting things wrong. World Rugby was petrified by that idea, because it didn't think ex-coaches and players had the necessary skillset. So the bunker officials are either former or active referees, which means World Rugby has just passed the decision making on to people who, in general, aren't as experienced as the referee on the pitch.

There's an element of Wizard of Oz about the bunker, in that when you pull the curtain back, it's just someone sitting in a van. Yes, they get to see as many replays from as many different angles as they want, but they don't possess magical powers, they're just someone with an opinion.

14

Complex Law

A perfect example of where the bunker would have come in handy was England full-back Freddie Steward's red card against Ireland in the 2023 Six Nations.

In case you don't remember, Ireland's Hugo Keenan stooped to gather a loose ball after his teammate knocked-on, Steward twisted his body as he braced for impact, and in doing so caught Keenan's head with his elbow, which was by his side. Keenan had to leave the pitch with concussion, and having reviewed the incident with his TMO Marius Jonker, Jaco Peyper dismissed Steward on the grounds that he had been reckless and upright as he came into 'highly dangerous contact' with Keenan.

It was a very controversial decision, with some people (mostly Ireland fans, including TV pundits Brian O'Driscoll and Rory Best) saying that Jaco had got it right, but with far more people calling his decision ridiculous. What else, they argued, could Steward have done? And when a disciplinary committee reviewed the incident a week later, they downgraded the card to a yellow. They still thought Steward had been reckless, but also that the 'late change in the dynamics and positioning' of Keenan needed to be considered.

When all the international referees got together after the tournament, we were shown the clip of Steward's sending-off and asked what we would have done. Interestingly, thirteen said no foul play had occurred, thirteen said they'd have given a yellow card, and no one said they would have given a red. But that was with the benefit of hindsight, and after the disciplinary committee had changed the decision, so it's no criticism of Jaco.

Contrary to what some people think, referees don't like sending players off, but there's pressure on us to do so. For the last few years, it's been drummed into us that if a player hits someone in the head, you've got to come down hard on it. So Jaco obviously thought, *Steward's not making a tackle, he's hit Keenan on the head, Keenan's had to go off with concussion, and I've been told to come down hard on this sort of thing. How do I not send him off?*

I'm writing this on the eve of the World Cup, so readers will know better than me how the bunker system played out. But the controversy surrounding Owen Farrell's sending off in England's warm-up game against Wales wasn't a great omen.

When I saw the incident – England captain Farrell tackled Wales's Taine Basham high – I thought it warranted a red card, so I wasn't surprised when the bunker official upgraded the referee's on-field yellow. But when the red card was rescinded after Farrell's disciplinary hearing, meaning a potential six-match ban was wiped out, I think most people, not just us refs, were taken aback.

It was the first time many fans had seen the bunker in action and the official had been overruled. England's World Cup-winning head coach Sir Clive Woodward said it made rugby 'a complete and utter laughing stock', while Progressive Rugby, which campaigns for better player protection, called the decision 'astounding.' Rugby had shot itself in the foot, again.

I know there was a lot going on in the background. Luckily, at least for us refs, World Rugby decided they needed to protect the integrity of the game, appealed the decision and got Farrell's red card reinstated. The right decision had finally been arrived at, but it looked like a fudge.

World Rugby's intervention didn't even put the controversy to bed. Tonga's George Moala had just received a five-match ban for a tip tackle against Canada, which led to accusations that it was one rule for tier 1 nations and another for tier 2 nations.

But while it's true that Moala had an exemplary disciplinary record, while Farrell had been previously sent off, I'd argue that Farrell's tackle, which appeared accidental and resulted in no injury to Basham, was very different to Moala's, which actually injured the bloke he tackled. Just as in the wider world, there has to be a link between the damage done and the harshness of the penalty.

Where I do think tier 1 nations are at a disadvantage is in their legal representation. Richard Smith is bloody good at what he does, and as one of the country's top silks, he won't come cheap. It reflects wider society, where the rich can afford the best lawyers money can buy while most people just have to muddle through.

I understand why we need to change players' behaviour when it comes to head injuries. We want fewer of them, naturally, and the authorities are very nervous about litigation. The main solution is encouraging players to tackle lower – and if they don't tackle lower, punish them. But not everything that results in an injury is illegal, and there's a big difference between deliberately smashing into someone's head with your shoulder and accidentally hitting someone on the head with your elbow while trying to get out of the way.

After the 2023 Six Nations, World Rugby gave us some guidance around hand-offs, essentially saying that if players get a hand-off slightly wrong, and they end up catching a defender's face with a forearm, they should be sent off. My immediate reaction was, 'That's a disaster waiting to happen and that directive will change after a big incident.'

Another directive that has come full circle in the space of a year is clamping down on defenders tackling over the shoulder, to try and hold a player up over the line.

In the first Test between New Zealand and Ireland in 2022, Irish replacement Joey Carbery was going for the line and a defender did exactly as I've described. Karl Dickson was the ref and I was a touch judge, and I could sense the TMO was going to try to talk us into giving a penalty try. But I thought, *Hold on a second, he hasn't touched his head or neck, so how is it foul play? It's just someone trying to get over the ball and prevent the attacker from scoring.* Karl and I had a chat, he agreed with me and gave a knock-on.

But afterwards, Ireland made it known how annoyed they were about the lack of a penalty try, and World Rugby, which is always reacting to team complaints rather than taking the lead, put the word out that it should have been given.

Subsequently, it was bombarded with clips of defenders stopping attackers from scoring by grabbing them over the shoulder, accompanied by words to the effect of, 'This is ridiculous, that's the only way the defender could have stopped him.' Then, at the start of 2023, World Rugby told us to forget about what it had said before and only award a penalty try if the defender makes contact with the head or neck.

Sometimes, rugby officials don't know if they're coming or going. Refs, touch judges and TMOs must be allowed to apply common sense and when necessary say, 'Yes, he's hit that person on the head and yes, he may have concussed him. But there's nothing he could have done about it. He is totally legal.'

Focusing on outcomes will inevitably lead to miscarriages of justice. And it's also why, in the aftermath of the Steward sending-off, we refs took things by the scruff of the neck and said, 'We need to remind people that accidentally hitting people in the head isn't an offence. Foul play is the offence, and for something to constitute foul play, a player needs to have actually done something wrong.'

What is often forgotten is that two-thirds of concussions are suffered by the tackler, not the ball carrier, almost always because they get their head on the wrong side and/or catch a knee to the head.

The dilemma rugby's lawmakers have is that lowering the height of the tackle can make the game less safe for the tackler. Even if you say that the tackler should aim to make contact on or below the ball carrier's midriff, the tackler only has to get it slightly wrong and suddenly they are at risk of cracking their head against hard, bony parts of the ball carrier's body, primarily knees and hips.

I recently listened to an interesting podcast with video assistant referees in football. They were saying that they try to deliver what they think is the *best* decision, not necessarily what they think is the *right* decision.

For example, if a defender makes slight contact with an attacker, the VAR officials will ask did the attacker really need to go down? Maybe the *technically correct* decision would be to award a penalty, but the *best* decision – the one most people would agree with – might be to wave play on. That's how difficult it is for referees in football and rugby, in that they're trying to make decisions based on what lots of other people, with lots of different opinions, think.

A big problem is that there's no overriding philosophy of how rugby referees should officiate a game. There's this vague notion that they should just referee the clear and obvious, but what's clear and obvious to one person isn't clear and obvious to another. Should a referee aim to keep a game moving? Should they aim to keep thirty players on the pitch? If we knew, it would help standardise decision making. As it was, I had to come up with my own philosophy, which was based on keeping the momentum of a game going.

I wanted quick scrums and scrum-halfs to hurry up their box kicks. I wanted to make quicker TMO decisions, which meant using as few replays as possible. I wanted substitutions to take place as someone was kicking a goal, not after he'd kicked it and he was running back to his own half. If the defence was all over the ball at the breakdown, I wanted to come down hard on them, because I thought that would give the attacking team the opportunity to play.

Sometimes, I felt moved to take matters into my own hands. For example, before the group game between New Zealand and Argentina at Wembley, I said to my video referee, an Aussie called George Ayoub, 'I know what we've been told about not doing TMO referrals on the run, but bollocks to it. Let's let things flow and avoid stopping things too often.'

George agreed, it was an amazing game, and the bosses congratulated me afterwards, which told me they didn't really know what they wanted.

I recently attended a shape-of-the-game conference in London, along with club owners, chief execs, directors of rugby and head coaches, and there was lots of talk about how to speed up the game. I emphasised that rugby should be asking refs to make fewer decisions and putting more pressure on teams. For example, I'd trial a shot clock, or whatever you wanted to call it. So if the ball was kicked into touch and the lineout wasn't taken within a given time, the other team would get the ball back. If you stuck it on the screen, like they do in other sports, it would be part of the entertainment for the fans.

TV execs and some more forward-thinking administrators are always going on about wanting 'more game', which means fewer stoppages. In other words, they want the product to be as attractive as possible. But club owners and coaches want officials to get every single decision right – whether it's a little knock-on, a marginal high tackle or an iffy bind in the scrum – which means a referee blowing their whistle even more often.

The coaches don't help, because after some games I'd be inundated with clips of stuff I supposedly got wrong. Sometimes I'd say to them, 'You've sent me thirty clips and the other coach has sent me twenty – did you really want me to stop the game another fifty times?' They would usually tell me not to be silly, but it highlights one of the main problems with rugby: a whistle-happy referee is one man's pleasure and another man's poison, while the reverse could be said for a referee like me, who likes to blow my whistle a little less often.

In international rugby, referees are marked on non-decisions as well as errors. And if you're going to get a cross against your name every time you don't make a decision, you're naturally going to make more decisions. It doesn't matter if not blowing your whistle will make for a better spectacle, you're more afraid of those crosses against your name, especially if there's a World Cup on the horizon.

To be fair to the RFU, it has invested in nine full-time referees, and one of those will be assigned to most Premiership games. We're the only group of referees in the world that gets together every week to discuss things, and while we don't have the same amount of time to prepare and review as we do for internationals, we've got something close to a team philosophy: don't blow your whistle unless you really have to; keep the game going and make decisions on the field, knowing that the TMO will back you up.

At times it feels as if World Rugby just wants a referee to get every little decision correct. They also appear to change interpretations and directives at the drop of a hat when a coach of one of the leading teams makes a complaint.

In the case of the tackling-over-the-shoulder directive, Ireland's coaches raised it with Joël and his management team and the directive was changed. But when people complained again, Joël had another chat with his team and decided to change it back again.

When Wales toured South Africa in summer 2022, you had a situation where Wales were defending the maul by putting one arm around the ball carrier and the other arm on the floor, almost like an American football three-point stance. It allowed them to get slightly lower and gain more purchase.

In the past, referees had mostly said, 'As long as you've got one arm on the maul, that's fine,' but South Africa didn't like it as it was disrupting one of their biggest weapons. They complained to World Rugby, saying the Welsh defenders didn't have their head above their hips and weren't supporting their weight, and we were told mid-series to start refereeing it.

I didn't understand that at all. First, should the people in charge be changing laws on the hoof in reaction to complaints from disgruntled coaches? Secondly, if a team manages to stop a maul, as long as they haven't deliberately dragged it down, they've done well!

Something else a couple of teams raised before the 2023 World Cup was pre-emptive movement at the lineout. Technically, lineout jumpers aren't allowed to start moving until the ball has been thrown, but you'll often see the two rear players start running on the hooker's backswing, if you will, so they're in a position to smash the ball carrier and get the maul moving forward. Again, it just seems like we're constantly looking for more reasons for a referee to blow their whistle and stop the game, and I envisaged lots of lineout free-kicks, especially in the early games.

The people who often get forgotten when it comes to the law are the players. Having spoken to some, I get the impression they just want to be kept in the loop. They know there are lots of grey areas, they just want to know what to expect from me, what they can or can't do at any given moment, or why I've made certain decisions. While they crave consistency, I do sometimes have to point out that consistency is difficult when two teams are involved. At the same time, they should know that my philosophy will be applied equally.

If a player asks me a question, I'll try to answer it. I'll certainly never turn my back or walk away (unless they've asked me the same question five or six times!). If I can see a player is about to commit an offence, I'll try to talk to them, rather than watch them do it and then blow my whistle.

Unlike coaches, club owners and World Rugby, players would rather I let the odd thing go if that means they get a free-flowing, exciting game. A couple of years ago, we were told to come down hard on attacking players rolling with the ball after being tackled, to prevent an opposition player from picking it up. But it was often difficult to tell if a player was deliberately rolling or had been sent into a roll by the tackle. I thought, *Why are we penalising players for this? The defence has done nothing to earn this turnover.* Or an attacking player might enter a ruck off his feet and I'd be expected to give a penalty, even though he didn't have any effect on play. I don't think most players care about a referee giving those kinds of decisions, and neither do I.

The one law the general public still get very agitated about is the crooked scrum feed. But players don't give a damn.

According to the law book, the scrum-half is still supposed to put the ball into the scrum straight, but over the years, the feeds got more and more crooked and not much noise was made about it. The only person who used to complain about it was former IRB chairman Syd Millar, who would bring it up every time he came to speak to the referees. We would be shown clips of crooked feeds and we'd all be smirking. Usually, someone would say, 'Do you really mean this?' World Rugby would say they did, then you'd watch the first game of the Six Nations and there wouldn't be a straight feed for the whole eighty minutes.

There was one young English ref called Greg Garner who'd been told to give a free-kick for the first crooked feed and a penalty for the second and third. If the scrum-half did it a fourth time, Greg was told to sinbin them. One game, Greg did what he was told and everyone was aghast – 'What the hell are you doing? You can't penalise a scrum-half for not putting the ball in straight, you're spoiling the game.'

The crooked feed has long been a bugbear of former England hooker Brian Moore, but you have to remember that when Brian was playing, they used to cheat in lots of other ways. You'd get hookers using their heads to hook the ball, which was illegal, but no one took much notice. Hookers would boot their opposite number in the shin, props would do all sorts of horrible things to each other. And after the game, they'd all laugh about it in the bar.

Organically, the game decided it wanted the ball to be in and out of the scrum as quickly as possible. That doesn't mean scrums are no longer contests, like in rugby league – just look at how England's scrum got beaten up by South Africa in the 2019 World Cup final – it just means they're no longer about the hook as much as they used to be.

And it's not as if hookers have been rendered redundant, they just have a different skillset. England's Jamie George can still hook and throw a ball, but he also has to be pretty good around the park.

And while it gets spoken about more than any other subject when I do Q & As, to the extent that I usually say, 'Just one rule – no questions about the scrum feed,' the people who get het up about it tend to be the generation above me. I'm not sure you'll find anyone below a certain age, or who actually plays the game, who gives a toss.

Too often, rugby forgets that not everyone who watches big games, especially World Cups, is a hardcore rugby fan. There will be people watching who won't have the foggiest idea what's going on, or why the referee keeps blowing his or her whistle. Consequently, they won't be coming back in a hurry. So the powers that be really need to start thinking, *What are we trying to achieve? Do we want refs to get every detail right, or do we want to make the sport as popular as possible by giving fans what they want, which is a fast-flowing game?*

World Rugby tried to slim down the law book a few years ago, but there are still twenty-one laws, and each of those laws has sub-laws. For example, the ruck law has nineteen. What the law book doesn't contain is an overriding principle, which should be, 'Keep the game going by blowing your whistle as little as possible.'

Referees should be marked down every time they stop a game when they don't need to. And while coaches should be able to present any concerns to referees, referees should be able to say to them, 'You're probably right by the letter of the law, but it's overridden by the principle of keeping the game going.'

My most controversial opinion on the law, and the one that often gets chucked back at me, is that attack and defence shouldn't be treated equally. I believe that attack should be refereed more leniently because most people want to see attacking rugby matches, not boring arm wrestles. I don't mean that good defence shouldn't be rewarded, I just mean that if you've got any doubt as a referee, give the attack the benefit.

Too many people in rugby are misty-eyed about a glorious past that never was. The ball might have been thrown and fed straight, but was the actual rugby any good? The stats suggest not. People wax lyrical about the 1973 New Zealand–Barbarians game – some still say it was the greatest game of rugby ever played – but somebody crunched the numbers and discovered that the ball was in play for nineteen minutes. That's a lot of lineouts and scrums.

In contrast, when Ireland played France in the 2023 Six Nations, the ball was in play for forty-seven minutes. I know what kind of game I'd prefer to watch.

The best way to stop a referee from blowing their whistle for eighty minutes isn't by fiddling with the laws, it's by upskilling everybody involved – refs, players and coaches – to make better decisions.

Even before I refereed that classic between Ireland and France in the 2023 Six Nations, I knew I was going to have a positive scrum day, and therefore fewer stoppages than normal, because they are two very well-coached teams with front rows who want to stay upright. But I went into other games knowing it was going to be a shitshow, because the stats told me so.

And after the game, when everyone was going on about what a terrible spectacle it was, what with all the collapsed and reset scrums, I'd think, *That had nothing to do with me.*

15

Europe

I never forgot that the English Premiership was the most watched league in the world – after I refereed a game that was on TV, I'd get messages from people in Australia and New Zealand – so I always wanted to put in a top-notch performance. I never wanted people to be able to criticise me. If a player messes up, whether they miss a crucial kick or drop the ball over the line in a cup final, it's soon forgotten about. But every single time you referee a game, your credibility is at stake. If you make an error, suddenly people will think you're terrible at your job. That's why I'm so proud that I was chosen to referee ten Premiership finals, because it means that for ten seasons I didn't make too many errors and the selectors thought I was the best.

But if I'm being brutally honest, refereeing club games was a bit of a grind for the last three or four years of my career.

I must have done something like 260 Premiership matches, as well as running touch, so it became more and more difficult to get myself up for a Sunday game in Newcastle in February, when there was snow on the ground, sideways sleet, and I could have been kicking a ball about with my kids in the back garden.

A big reason I kept refereeing for so long were the European trips, which were like sumptuous feasts in among the bread and butter of Premiership rugby.

There would be four of us in some amazing French or Italian city and we'd always be able to find ourselves a nice cosy restaurant and bar. One of my favourite cities is Toulouse, which has three UNESCO World Heritage sites, beautiful weather and some of the best gastronomy in France. One of the few drawbacks is that the locals really don't like it when their team loses.

I refereed Toulouse's Heineken Cup game against Glasgow in 2009, when Glasgow caused one of the biggest upsets in the tournament's history. Prior to that day, Toulouse hadn't lost at the Stade Ernest-Wallon in two years, while Glasgow had never beaten a French side away from home. Toulouse kicked a late consolation penalty, and I blew my whistle while running towards the tunnel, leaving my touch judges under the posts with their flags in the air. I said to them before I legged it, 'Fellas, see you in the changing room . . .'

That night, we went to a bar owned by Trevor Brennan, the former Ireland and Toulouse player. We were having a few quiet beers when the entire Glasgow team filed in, which was when those few quiet beers turned into a colossal piss-up. Scotland back row Kelly Brown got his guitar out and soon I was singing along with my arm around him. That's when Toulouse's legendary head coach Guy Novès suddenly appeared with his family in tow. Novès shot me a look of contempt and I contemplated never refereeing Toulouse again.

Something similar happened after Toulon played Munster in the semi-finals of the Heineken Cup in 2014. Toulon won a decent game, with no controversy, and afterwards we headed into Marseille for a few beers. We were in an Irish bar in the old port when someone chucked a Munster top at me and asked me to put it on. Being quite oiled, and Munster having lost, I agreed. That wasn't very bright because, at some point in the evening, Toulon's head coach Bernard Laporte walked in. I have no idea what Laporte was doing in an Irish bar at midnight after a game – I thought a Michelin-starred restaurant was more his style – but it was another excruciatingly embarrassing moment.

When you got to the knockout stages of the European Cup, most games would be of international standard, especially if it was a French derby or a game between an Irish and a French team. The first half an hour of 2023's semi-final between Leinster and Toulouse was one of the most intense periods of rugby I've ever been involved in.

Those French derbies were particularly difficult to handle because French refs have a different way of doing things. I'd try my best to referee those games how European and World Rugby expected the game to be refereed, instead of how it would be refereed in the Top 14. That would mean even more preparation than usual, and saying to the coaches, 'Look, you need to get the message across to your players that this is a European game, not a league game.'

I had French lessons once a week, and after a game involving French teams, a fellow referee would watch the game and say stuff like, 'Next time, you might want to put it this way instead, you're getting your *tu*s and *vous* mixed up.' (I once asked a scrum-half to put the ball into the washing machine instead of scrum.)

On the day of the game, I'd seek out English speakers on either team, usually those I knew from internationals, in the hope they'd be able to help me out if things got messy during the game. Those players were also more likely to know my style of refereeing and adapt accordingly. But I'd still do my front-row briefings in French, because that was the respectful thing to do. Sometimes, I'd have to stop and say, 'Mate, you might have to help me out with this bit,' but I think they appreciated that I was at least giving it a crack.

However much preparation I did, I'd still have to be strong in those first few minutes, because places like Clermont, Pau and Bourgoin back in the day could be bloody intimidating. I'd often find myself saying things like, 'Fellas, you can't scrummage like that!' or 'Fellas, you can't be attacking the breakdown when you've got players on the wrong side!' And I'd just have to cross my fingers that, at some point, the penny would drop.

— ★ —

I refereed three European Cup finals, in 2010, 2018 and 2022. The first was a shitshow of a game between Biarritz and Toulouse, played in ridiculous heat in Paris. If I'd been more experienced, I might have been able to force them to play a bit more, but at least I was barely mentioned in dispatches.

The second was between Leinster and Racing 92 in Bilbao, which was the first time the final had been played outside the Six Nations countries. San Mamés is where Athletic Bilbao play their home games and it's such a cool stadium, but once again it wasn't the greatest of spectacles, with Leinster winning five penalties to four in wet conditions.

Fortunately, my last final, La Rochelle v. Leinster in Marseille, made up for the first two, at least in terms of excitement. That was a phenomenal occasion, with colour and noise galore, and it got the ending it deserved, replacement La Rochelle wing Arthur Retière going over for the winning try in the final minute.

But at the risk of sounding ungrateful, I'll look back on my European career with a touch of disappointment. When I decided to carry on after the 2019 World Cup, one of the reasons was that I hadn't refereed as many European Cup finals as I thought I could have, considering how long I'd been doing the job. Almost every time a final came around, either an English team was in it or it was promised to someone else for sentimental reasons.

In 2008, it was me and Nigel Owens in the frame for Munster v. Toulouse, but I was told that because it was at the

Millennium Stadium, and Nige might never get the chance to referee a final in Cardiff again, he was getting the gig.

Then there was Toulon v. Clermont in Dublin, 2013. I'd been told I was in the shake-up, based on my performances that season, but the selection board was a bit like Eurovision in that all six countries had a representative and the Celtic countries would vote *en bloc* for one of their guys. Ireland's Alain Rolland had also never refereed a final in Dublin and was coming towards the end of his career, so they give it to him instead.

Saracens played in four of the next six finals, before Exeter reached the final in 2020. I finally got that third final in 2022, but I was disappointed not to get the rematch in 2023. They told me it wouldn't make sense to have the same ref for the same teams two years in a row, but I just thought, *If I'm the best man for the job, and you know I'm retiring, why not pick me?* They gave the gig to Jaco Peyper instead, and I must say, he's a fantastic referee, and being the first ever South African to referee the final meant the world to him.

Some people think that once you start refereeing internationals, you no longer get more obscure appointments, but that isn't the case. Saying that, I'm not quite sure how I ended up running touch in the equivalent of the county championship final in France, which took place in a small town just outside Toulouse.

If I remember rightly, I'd been an assistant ref for a Heineken Cup game in Clermont-Ferrand, so when one of the French officials dropped out, I was asked to fill in, which I was only too happy to do. It took me four hours to get there, and when I arrived, I was greeted by members of the Midi-Pyrénées committee, who whisked me straight to a restaurant for a five-course meal, with wine and champagne.

The following day, I turned up to the ground and discovered that neither of the other match officials spoke a word of English. The game itself was all-out warfare, which I was told was quite normal for that level of rugby in France. It took me right back to my early days refereeing in the Forest of Dean.

Talking of France, one of my favourite games of all time was London French v. Kilburn Cosmos, not long after the 2015 World Cup. I was meant to be reffing Stade Français v. Munster, but the game was called off because of the terrorist attacks in Paris. I could have put my feet up for the weekend, but instead I rang up the local referee society and asked if I could do a game in London.

On my way to the ground in Barnes, which is just around the corner from my place in Twickenham, I thought about what a veteran ref from London, a guy called Roger Quittenton, had once told me: 'Every game you referee could be their biggest game of the season, so take it as seriously as you would a World Cup final.'

Before kick-off, everyone was invited on to the pitch to share in a moment's silence, and then the London French chairman said a few words. The captain of Cosmos presented his opposite number with a bouquet of flowers in the colours of the French tricolour, which was a classy moment.

The game itself was played in a great spirit, and when I still hadn't given a penalty after ten minutes, I thought, *I wonder if I can get through eighty minutes without giving one?* There were quite a few borderline incidents and I reflexively raised my whistle to my lips, but I managed to resist the temptation to blow, which was the only time that happened in my career.

After the game, I was greeted in the clubhouse by London French's chairman, who presented me with a club beret and a glass of Chablis, which was pretty special. I also got man of the match, along with a player from each team, and had to stand on a chair with my beret on and neck a dirty pint.

16

Losing Control

For reasons I will never understand, Ireland decided to play a warm-up against Bayonne before the start of the 2007 World Cup.

Ireland had been drawn in the same group as France, and the Bayonne players seemed quite keen to nobble a few of their star players, with Brian O'Driscoll the number-one target. It was vicious from the off, with Bayonne kicking the crap out of Ireland at every opportunity and me mopping up the carnage.

When we walked off at half-time, Ireland head coach Eddie O'Sullivan was going mad at me – 'It's a fucking disgrace! You've got to protect my players!' – and I thought, *Don't blame me if anyone gets hurt, blame the Irish RFU for organising this shitshow two weeks before a World Cup!*

After about an hour, O'Driscoll informed me his team-mates were being eye-gouged and threatened to walk off. I thought, *If you want to walk off, I'm not stopping you. I don't really want to be involved in this either.*

I'd already issued a few yellow cards when a bit of argy-bargy broke out and O'Driscoll hit the deck like a sack of spuds. The game wasn't even being filmed, so my touch judges and I had no idea what had happened (it was only after the game that grainy amateur footage emerged of O'Driscoll being punched by Kiwi lock Mikaera Tewhata). What we did know was that Ireland's talisman had sustained a nasty-looking injury on the eve of a World Cup and the whole ugly spectacle had been both inevitable and avoidable.

As it turned out, O'Driscoll's injury wasn't as bad as first feared and he played in all of Ireland's group games. Ireland almost lost to Georgia, however, and were well beaten by France and Argentina, meaning they didn't qualify for the quarter-finals. When the RFU presented me with my 100th cap, we had a little reception at Twickenham and they'd pulled together some messages of congratulations, including one from O'Driscoll. He just said, 'Barnesy, I've just about forgiven you for the match in Bayonne in 2007.'

Ironically, Ireland are playing another World Cup warm-up in Bayonne in 2023 – and I'm reffing it again! This time they're playing Samoa. I don't think we'll get another 'Battle of Bayonne', but it does seem to be tempting fate somewhat.

— ⋆ —

Despite the best efforts of rugby authorities and officials, rugby can never be made entirely safe. It has, however, got a lot less violent in the age of the TMO. When I started refereeing professionally, there would be lots of allegations of fingers in eyes, grabbing of testicles and biting, and sometimes I'd find myself thinking, *What on earth goes through people's minds that they think that's okay to do?* And the problem with that kind of stuff was that in the absence of multiple camera angles, it would often be impossible to prove.

Certain games would get out of control very quickly and all I could do was try to limit the damage. One of my first European fixtures was Italian side Rovigo against a French team and there were punch-ups breaking out all over the pitch. In a situation like that, I'd end up blowing very quickly every time there was a possible infringement, to prevent things spilling over. Or I'd say to my touch judges, 'You stay on the breakdown and I'll run with the ball,' because otherwise we were bound to miss some foul play.

I reffed Munster v. Leinster at Musgrave Park in Cork, in about 2008, when their rivalry was at its peak, and at one point I had to bring all the forwards together and say, 'This is getting silly. You have to stop kicking each other.' An air of acceptance fell upon the group, as if they all thought, *Yeah, he's probably right, we've done enough damage already.*

Every now and again, I'd get a decision horribly wrong, as happened in the Premiership semi-final between Leicester and Northampton in 2011. Leicester's Manu Tuilagi tackled Saints' Chris Ashton high, before Ashton shoved Tuilagi on the back of the head. Tuilagi then sprang to his feet and landed two left jabs on Ashton's chin, followed by a big overhand right. How Ashton stayed on his feet I do not know.

The problem was, this all happened behind my back, so I had to rely on my touch judge, who informed me that both players had thrown punches and recommended they both be sinbinned. When I saw the replay after the game, I felt a bit ridiculous: everyone watching on TV had seen Ashton do nothing much and Tuilagi almost take his head off, and I'd given both the same treatment.

Years later, I was at a corporate do with Ashton and he said to me, 'I've got a question for you, Barnesy: how the hell did I get a yellow card for Manu Tuilagi kicking the shit out of me?' I replied, 'Because you're Chris Ashton and I thought you probably deserved it.' We also chatted before the 2023 Premiership semi-final between Leicester and Sale. Ashton was meant to be playing for the Tigers, in what would have been his last hurrah, but because he'd been sent off in their last regular game of the season against Harlequins, and even though the independent panel did reduce his punishment to a yellow card, as the hearing was so close to the final, he wasn't even selected to be on the bench.

During the warm-up, Ashton sidled up to me and said, 'Barnesy, there's no way you would have sent me off for that tackle.' I replied, 'Mate, I would have sent you off and turned up to the hearing to make sure you got a very long ban.' I was joking, of course, because I'd have loved to have reffed his last ever game. He looked rueful and said, 'Barnesy, it just about sums up my career.'

But whatever happened in my pro career, nothing could have been worse than some of the games I reffed in amateur rugby. Whether it was a county cup game in the Forest of Dean, with punch-ups on the field and on the touchline, or a Norfolk local derby between Norwich and North Walsham, with all-in brawls breaking out all over the pitch, it was the best grounding you could possibly have as a ref.

Often, it's the noise that tells me I'm caught up in a game – or maybe just a moment – that people will talk about for a long time.

Towards the end of my career, I worked a lot with Christophe Ridley (born in Paris but an alumni of the University of Gloucestershire), Karl Dickson and Tom Foley, and we developed a strong team bond. So whenever one of us felt like we were in one of those 'moments' and feeling under a bit of pressure – maybe we'd just made a big decision and knew there'd be close-ups of us on millions of TVs and the commentators would be talking about said decision – we'd use a trigger word.

For example, if I've just yellow-carded a player and I know it hasn't gone down well with the rest of his team, and at least some of the fans, someone will say this trigger word and it will bring a smile to everyone's faces. But it's not about making light of things, it's more about helping us reset and refocus. Because once you've done that, you can get on with things knowing that you made the decision with the best information you had, rather than thinking, *Shit, that might have been a dodgy decision, maybe I need to give the other side a dodgy one to even things up and stop them from being so grumpy.*

In the second Test between Ireland and New Zealand in 2022, the All Blacks were shown two yellow cards and one red in the first half, with prop Angus Ta'avao being sent off for a head-first tackle on Garry Ringrose. Most people thought they were the right decisions, but in the lead-up to the third and deciding Test in Wellington, which I was refereeing, there was a lot of toing and froing with the coaches.

I suppose New Zealand head coach Ian Foster wanted to avoid a repeat of the previous week, while Ireland head coach Andy Farrell was worried about me yielding to home pressure and going too soft on the All Blacks. But I needed them to trust me, because that would make me more relaxed. And when a referee is more relaxed, they're more likely to make fair decisions.

Ireland were leading New Zealand a merry old dance and looking like comfortable winners when Brodie Retallick was whacked on the head by Andrew Porter after fifty minutes. The fans wanted – and expected – me to give Porter a red card, but we thought he had just been a bit clumsy and wasn't active in the tackle. So instead of a red, I sent Porter to the sinbin.

We knew it was going to be a controversial decision with the crowd, owing to what had happened the previous week. Because Ta'avao had been red-carded and Porter only sinbinned, they'd convinced themselves that there was some kind of conspiracy against them. I had nothing to do with the second Test – that was a different refereeing team – but we knew from all the booing and jeering that we were now in a bit of a tense situation. That's where the trigger word came in.

During the week, Christophe, Karl, Tom and I had been chatting about karate quite a lot, because Christophe used to do it and my two kids had just got their brown belts. And Christophe kept threatening to use a karate phrase and a move if things got pressured. While we were waiting for the dust to settle, Christophe mumbled 'kiai' into his microphone and we all broke into big grins. But then I remembered Christophe's threat and thought, *Mate, don't be doing anything daft like a spinning roundhouse kick* . . . To my relief, he opted for the basic karate chop. Not really, but I kind of wish he had.

That was our team saying, 'Look, we're in a tough game, and we've just made a decision that has upset a few people, but let's just park it and crack on.' And it was one of those special shared moments we'll always remember.

Lots of situations in life are made easier if you share the angst around and try to make light of it. It doesn't necessarily mean you're not taking the situation seriously, it's just a way of coping.

As a rugby referee, as I've already emphasised, if spectators don't notice you, chances are you've done a decent job. It means you've got your preparation right, you've allowed the game to flow and you've made any big decisions in an unobtrusive way.

That's not easy to do, because a rugby referee is pulling strings left, right and centre and making hundreds of split-second decisions over the course of eighty minutes. And sometimes, especially in big games, it's simply not possible to stay under the radar because we're forced into making game-deciding decisions in the most obtrusive way possible, namely while we're up there on the big screen with 80,000 spectators watching, plus millions more at home.

Take the Six Nations game between France and Wales in 2017. I'd prepared as well as I could have done, and we all went for a meal the night before, which is always very pleasant in Paris. I was slightly concerned that I'd never worked with this particular TMO before, but I knew my two touch judges well. Plus, the local fourth and fifth officials seemed like good guys and spoke fluent English. Never has the phrase 'calm before the storm' seemed so applicable.

For the first seventy-odd minutes it was a pretty low-key game. France dominated the first half but kept giving away penalties and were only one point ahead at the break. And three more penalties from Leigh Halfpenny meant Wales led by five points with a minute to go, despite struggling in the scrum and rarely threatening the French line. Then it all went a bit wonky.

With the French camped on Wales's line, the atmosphere in the Stade de France had turned full gladiatorial. Then, after the third or fourth reset scrum, France's doctor ran on the pitch and asked prop Uini Atonio if he needed some water. Atonio said no, and when I asked him if he was injured, he said he had a sore back but was fine to continue. Watch it back and you'll notice my bemusement. Then, after yet another collapsed scrum, the same doctor reappeared and said Atonio had to go off to have a head-injury assessment.

When it comes to head injuries, a referee relies almost entirely on the word of the player and his doctor. So even if you suspect a player is feigning injury so that a fresher, more effective scrummager can replace him, there's nothing you can do about it.

So while Brian Moore was pretty much accusing France of cheating on commentary, all I could do was get the doctor to take responsibility for the decision – 'You're a doctor, so you're telling me this player is injured and needs a head-injury assessment?' – and follow his lead. So off went Atonio and on came Rabah Slimani – Atonio having replaced Slimani only twenty-five minutes earlier. I told you things can get complicated . . .

After untold conversations with players, doctors and officials – and with Wales defence coach Shaun Edwards going doolally on the touchline – the game finally restarted. But a minute later, I had to show Wales prop Samson Lee a yellow card for collapsing the scrum. After yet more tense conversations with my fourth and fifth official, which lasted two or three minutes and sounded like a scene from 'Allo! 'Allo!, I finally ascertained that Tomas Francis, who Lee had replaced twenty-odd minutes earlier, was allowed to re-enter the fray (had Francis been replaced because of an injury, I wouldn't have been able to let him back on and we would have had to continue with uncontested scrums).

There was no getting away from it, the game had turned into a bit of a farce, and I was a very reluctant headline act. Seven minutes into overtime, France were still camped on Wales's try line – and we still hadn't had an acceptable scrum. I was under tremendous pressure to award a penalty try, for repeated collapsing – the chat from French captain Yoann Maestri was constant – but I really didn't want to.

I'd prepared for all these scenarios in isolation. What I couldn't prepare for was all of them happening in quick succession, in overtime, in Paris, with 80,000 fans applying intense pressure, and fast-tiring players willing to do anything to win the match – while convinced I was out to cheat them.

After a couple of French attacks that came to nothing, Samson Lee came back on, his ten minutes in the sinbin over. As if things couldn't get any weirder, on ninety-three minutes, while I was warning Welsh captain Sam Warburton that I might have to sinbin another of his players for scrum infringements, a frantic George North came up to me and said he'd been bitten on the arm.

I could clearly see the bite mark, and George knew exactly where it had happened – after he was tackled by French full-back Bruce Dulin. But if I didn't see it, and the TMO couldn't see it on the replays, there was nothing we could do about it. For the next minute or so, it was just my face on the screen, while my TMO Peter Fitzgibbon trawled through the footage. I'm sure that was a very uncomfortable little period for one of those French players. But Peter couldn't find anything, so I had no choice but to get on with the game.

It's not like I didn't believe George – he was always one of the good guys and certainly not the kind of bloke who'd make up something like that – but referees can't find someone guilty without any evidence.

But as the clock ticked on, the match turned ever more farcical. At one point, I was told my fourth official had an issue. I blew my whistle to stop the scrum engaging, asked what the issue was – and was told there wasn't one.

By that stage, I was fast losing patience. You can see it in my face and hear it in my voice. We eventually got a half-decent scrum and France had a couple of snipes at the line. But as France prepared for another attack, Dan Biggar kicked the ball while lying on the floor and I had to announce that he'd be sent to the sinbin, as soon as the advantage was over. But I didn't need to show Biggar a yellow card because, a few seconds later, and five seconds short of 100 minutes, a French player lunged at the line and touched the ball down for a try. I had no idea who'd scored, and I really didn't care.

The TMO confirmed it was French number eight Damien Chouly who had burrowed over, and the crowd went wild. Camille Lopez kicked the winning conversion, before the crowd – and France's players – went even wilder. As for the Welsh, they just thought they'd been swindled.

Funnily enough, it was Yoann Maestri who ended up getting a hefty fine for criticising my performance. He accused me of being involved in some kind of 'Anglo-Saxon' conspiracy. That would have been news to the Welsh players, whose pride at their Celtic heritage is unsurpassed.

Wales head coach Rob Howley wasn't happy at the post-match dinner, but he was more upset about what he saw as French chicanery. In fact, Rob, his assistant Neil Jenkins and I had a calm, sensible conversation about it, and they accepted that my hands had been tied. Meanwhile, Shaun Edwards was following Atonio around all night, trying to see if he was drinking any alcohol, which you're not allowed to do if you've been concussed. At one point, Atonio left his drink on the table and Edwards started sniffing it.

As for me, I was irritated that my name was all over the media. And I couldn't help thinking, *Shit, could I have done better today?* But sometimes as a referee, you just have to accept that there was no way of avoiding it. Like the pilot of a plane, you hit an unexpected storm and you just have to battle through it.

In the 2012 Six Nations, it was France's turn to host Ireland in Paris, and I was assistant referee to Dave Pearson. The evening before the game, Dave carried out a pitch inspection at the Stade de France, and he didn't like what he saw. It had been a bitterly cold February and the pitch was frozen solid. But Dave thought that if it was covered, which the Fédération Française de Rugby (FFR) agreed to do, it might be playable.

Before France–Ireland, England played Italy in Rome. The ground staff had to clear the pitch of snow and scrape the lines, but they managed to get a game in. However, when we turned up to the Stade de France a few hours before the 9 p.m. kick-off, it was clear that they hadn't covered the whole pitch, because patches of it were still rock hard.

The regulations clearly state that if a pitch is frozen and dangerous, the game should be called off, but the FFR insisted they had time to fix it. So for a couple of hours, we watched forlornly as tiny blowers, which looked like the *Teletubbies* vacuum cleaner, were used in an attempt to defrost the pitch. The whole time I was thinking, *There's absolutely no way this match is happening.*

When the coaches Philippe Saint-André and Declan Kidney arrived, we showed them the pitch and they both agreed the game shouldn't go ahead. You might think the decision to cancel a game lies with someone on the Six Nations Committee, but it lies with the referee. However, we thought that if we had the coaches' backing, at least Dave could say it was a collective decision.

By the time we'd tracked down a Six Nations representative, crowds had started streaming through the turnstiles and filling the stands. We told the rep that the game couldn't go ahead, and that we had the coaches' backing, and she replied, 'Okay, but you'll have to tell the media.' When I'd finally picked my jaw off the floor, I said, 'What are you on about? We're not addressing the media, we're going to our changing room and locking the door.'

This Six Nations rep went off to tell the media, but still nothing had been announced at nine o'clock, by which time there were 80,000 very cold and confused people in the stadium, wondering why there were no teams on the pitch. Then, at 9.05, the two big screens at either end of the field flashed the message: THE REFEREE HAS DECIDED TO CALL THE GAME OFF DUE TO A FROZEN PITCH. That went down well, especially with the Irish contingent who'd shelled out hundreds of euros for the weekend.

While this was going on, we were hiding in our changing room, watching the farce play out on TV. Now I knew what it felt like for the defenders of the Bastille, just before it was stormed back in 1789. We knew we'd made the right decision, but that decision should have been relayed to the media and paying public about four hours earlier than it was, if not twenty-four hours.

Suddenly, there was an angry banging on the door. We'd told the security guard not to let anyone in, but he was new in the job and buckled after about twenty-five seconds. The door swung open and in burst the president of the FFR, Pierre Camou, closely followed by the treasurer. They were both puce-faced and almost frothing at the mouth, and because I was the only official who spoke any French, they directed their fury at me, and I translated for Dave.

Between the effing and jeffing, they kept insisting the pitch was playable, based on the fact the Italy–England game had gone ahead with a team of French officials. They seemed to be insinuating that while the French had done England a favour, us English refs had set out to ruin their game.

In hindsight, we should have gone straight to Camou as soon as we saw the state of the pitch, instead of him hearing about the cancellation second-hand. Maybe he'd have tried to talk us out of it, but at least he wouldn't have felt disrespected.

After soaking up this double-barrelled verbal attack for five minutes, Camou stormed off, leaving the even angrier treasurer behind. I asked him in my terrible French, 'Quitter notre vestiaire!' ('Leave our changing room!') To which he replied, 'Ce n'est pas votre vestiaire! C'est mon vestiaire! Je resterai aussi longtemps que je veux!' ('This is not your changing room! This is my changing room! I will stay as long as I want!').

By this time I was thinking, *Why am I getting all the blame? I'm just Dave's translator!* And in the end, I said, 'All right, this might be the only way to get rid of you . . .' before taking my kit off. He held his ground until I was down to my off-grey boxer shorts, which probably would have repelled the stormers of the Bastille. At that point, the treasurer flashed me a disgusted look, gestured indecipherably, turned on his heels and left, slamming the door behind him.

I said to the security guard, if you could call him that, 'We're locking the door now, please don't let anyone else in.' Two minutes later, there was another loud knocking, which grew louder and louder the longer we ignored it. After a tense few minutes, I said to Dave, 'We're gonna have to open it.' And when I did, there was a monster of a man filling the doorway. I gave the security guard a quizzical look, and he said to me, 'It's the Minister of Sports.'

This guy was a former heavyweight judo champion, and for a moment I thought he was going to tear the lot of us limb from limb. As it turned out, he was the most sympathetic of all of them. I explained that the game had been called off because of player safety, and he said he understood. I later found out that he went straight to the FFR guys and gave them an almighty bollocking about the stadium's lack of underground heating and covering. Oh, to have been a fly on the wall . . .

17

Fit for Purpose

I don't enjoy fitness training and never really have. However hard I try, I'm never going to be one of the fittest, which is probably why I'm cynical about the need for fitness testing.

When I first came on the scene, referees' fitness wasn't taken as seriously as it is now. As long as you weren't lardy and could keep up with play, that was enough.

Spreaders's pre-match warm-up was brushing his hair. Welsh referee Derek Bevan was fifty-two when he refereed at the 1999 World Cup. No wonder those old refs would cheat like buggery in tests. By the end of the dreaded bleep test, the cones between which they ran, which were supposed to be twenty metres apart, would be eighteen metres apart. Back then, it wasn't just about being the fittest, it was also about being the smartest, which I quite admire.

I'm told that before the 2003 World Cup, the refs had to do sixty-metre sprints – in a sports hall that wasn't sixty metres long. That meant they had to do the sprints diagonally and make very sharp turns so that they didn't go flying into the Coca-Cola vending machine that was positioned in one corner. As a result, three of the refs pulled calf or thigh muscles.

I've always been reasonably fit and kept injury-free, though I did have a little issue with my heart back in 2009. I should have known something was off when I reffed the Lions v. Free State Cheetahs, up at altitude in Bloemfontein. When I came off the pitch, I looked at my heart-rate watch and the reading was through the roof. But I felt like I'd worked particularly hard that game, and I also wondered if my watch was dodgy.

When I got home, I'd do my warm-up run to the gym at Twickenham, which is less than a mile away from my house, and be really blowing by the time I got there. I just thought I hadn't slept properly. But then when I did a bleep test at Bath University, my heart rate was about 150 bpm just a few minutes in, and I was still only at the fast walking stage. When I reached level five, which is when you start jogging, I had to stop, because I was absolutely knackered. Our doctor Simon Kemp checked my pulse and immediately said, 'Your heart's not beating right.' That's not really what you want to hear.

Kempy went off to find a heart-rate monitor, but the only thing he could find was a defibrillator. He assured me it would do the job and started sticking pads on my chest.

Up to that point, he really looked like he knew what he was doing. But then I noticed Kempy looking at this defibrillator rather quizzically. When I asked him what was up, he said, 'I'm not sure what button to press.'

'Hold on, Kempy,' I replied. 'So what you're saying is, if you press the right button, we'll get a heart reading? But if you press the wrong button, you'll shock my heart and maybe kill me?' Kempy just nodded.

Rather than take the risk, we decided I should go to a local GP's surgery instead. But by the time I got there, my heart was beating normally again. The same happened when I went to see a cardiologist, but he decided to put a monitor on me for forty-eight hours, which showed something was indeed up.

When I saw a consultant, he diagnosed something called atrial fibrillation, which basically means that your heart will suddenly start beating erratically because of misfiring electrodes (I'm sure a doctor would give you a more scientific explanation). I was then introduced to a phenomenal guy called Richard Schilling, who recommended something called ablation, which involves inserting a wire through your groin, then into your heart, and incinerating the misfiring electrodes (again, Richard might put it slightly differently).

Richard said I'd be almost back to normal after four weeks, but when I read the terms and conditions, one of them was that the operation could kill me, which made me somewhat less keen to sign up. I went back to Richard and said, 'Can I just talk to you about these Ts and Cs. I noticed one of the possible side-effects is death . . .' To which Richard replied, 'Oh yes, don't worry about that, you'll be fine. We just have to put that in for your lawyers.'

Right before the op, which took place on 23 December 2009, a nurse walked into my room and said, 'Do you know what a Brazilian is?' I was too tongue-tied to reply. After an awkward pause, she smiled, handed me some clippers and said, 'You can sort yourself out . . .'

They can't give you a general anaesthetic for an ablation because your heart needs to be beating normally, so I woke up halfway through. I was in excruciating pain and making some terrible noises, until Richard turned up the sedation dial and knocked me out again.

Richard was right: I didn't die. But there were a couple more indignities. The following morning, I was in the shower when I noticed that the incision was nowhere near where my pubic hair should have been, so I'd gone Brazilian for nothing. And when I was washing my bum, I felt some dressing, started pulling it and, about two metres later, this dressing was still coming. The next time I saw Richard, I said, 'Why was all that dressing up my backside?' Richard replied, 'I've no idea. I didn't put it there.' That's when I started thinking that maybe the nurse had been a Kiwi.

I spent the next few days in Bream with my leg elevated, being waited on hand and foot. I'll never forget that Christmas, not just because of the op, but also because my mum bought me and Polly a steam iron. Which is, of course, what every young and madly in love couple wants. Less than two months later, I was refereeing France v. Ireland in the second round of the Six Nations.

In contrast to the old days of referees who bent the rules and had dicky tickers, some of the lads I train with now are off the scale in terms of fitness. And few are fitter than Karl Dickson, who played almost 300 games of professional rugby before becoming a referee and is a CrossFit devotee.

One of the tests we have to do is skinfold, to check how fat we are, because they don't want podgy refs running around the field. They usually take skinfold measurements from four parts of the body, and Karl's four measurements added up to less than my love handle.

We've had so many different World Rugby trainers over the course of my career, and it always tends to be people who would much rather be training players than referees. When our current trainer, who's an Irish chap, took over, he said, 'I want you lot to feel comfortable refereeing with your tops off.' That was the extent of his ambition for us. But there were still a few of us looking at each other, shaking our heads and smirking at the ridiculousness of it.

Before the 2019 World Cup, we had a Kiwi trainer who thought it would be a good idea to introduce the maximum chin-up test (because referees famously do a lot of chin-ups during a game). I took a run and jump, Karl gave me a lift halfway up and I was still only able to do one. He then added the maximum bench press, so Karl spent a lot of time in the gym saving me from having my chest caved in. One day I asked, 'Why are we doing this?' And the guy said, 'We need to measure your power . . .' For what, he couldn't say.

As for running, we've had all sorts of tests over the years, ranging from the good old bleep to the Yo-Yo. The one we do now is the Bronco, which involves running twenty metres to the line and back, forty metres to the line and back, sixty metres to the line and back, five times without stopping. I'm told New Zealand's Beauden Barrett does it in about 4 minutes 15 seconds, and one of our refs, Christophe Ridley, did it in 4:18. That's the kind of athlete we have among us.

Before our most recent trainer took over, my best was 4:59, which meant I passed by a second. But when this new guy looked at our results, he decided to lower the pass threshold to 4:50. I said to him, 'Well, I'll never pass then. I couldn't even do that four years ago.' He replied, 'Wayne, it's just a number.'

I didn't get very good marks in the other three tests either, which are sprints, skinfolds and, hilariously, how high we can jump. In fact, I scored zero out of ten, and while I did better second time around, scoring one and a half, I still failed. I said to the trainer, 'Mate, are you trying to pension me off?' He replied, 'No, we're just setting the bar really high.' I always try to peak at a World Cup, so I'll have trained intensively in the lead-up, but the chances of me ever passing that test are precisely nil.

Look, I understand the endurance test, because referees are on the move for eighty minutes. But it would make more sense if they tailored the endurance test to how long the ball is normally in play for (when it's continuously in play for four minutes, which happens nowadays, it's lung-busting). And it would help if the GPS data told me something other than how far I ran in a match (between seven and eight kilometres is the norm, which is usually more than any player other than the scrum-halfs). As for the other stuff, I'll never understand why we need to jump high, do even a single chin-up or have less flabby triceps.

During our World Rugby camps, which can be in either hemisphere, we regularly end up doing maximum sprints within twelve hours of landing. I once put my hand up and said, 'Is this really wise? We've just had a twenty-four-hour trip.' I was told to get on with it.

The really farcical part about all this is that the 2015 and 2019 World Cup finals were refereed by Nigel Owens and Jérôme Garcès respectively. Nige was never exactly known for his fleetness of foot and I've seen milk turn quicker than Jérôme. But their fitness and manoeuvrability were deemed less important than their refereeing prowess, and rightly so.

A trainer who used to be employed by Fulham FC joined the RFU on a part-time basis about 10 years ago, and she understands that while they need fit referees, we don't have to be competing with the players. So her focus is on keeping us robust and stopping us from getting injured, which I think is smart.

I do most of my training at the gym at Twickenham Stadium, which is usually empty apart from me. Until three or four years ago, we had to do all our running on a strip of artificial grass than runs adjacent to the West Stand. It's about three metres wide. But because we complained so much, they eventually let us use a patch of grass in the West car park. Talk about knowing your place in the pecking order! Whenever we trained on the Monday after a game, it would be covered in cigarette butts and beer cans.

But when I've got my headphones on, I'm like Rocky in one of those training montages. Or at least I'm able to convince myself I am. Absolute Radio 80s got me through the 2019 World Cup, and if I have the Twickenham gym to myself, I'll ditch the headphones and stick some Elaine Paige on the stereo. There's nothing like a bit of *Evita* to get you in the mood. Whenever I was in the gym with Nigel Owens, he'd insist on listening to hymns and arias. Sometimes, I'd look up and see him pumping iron to the strains of 'Bread of Heaven'.

No doubt about it, ex-players have a big advantage when it comes to refereeing, and not just because of their fitness. By the time Karl Dickson, for example, refereed his first Premiership game, he'd already been involved in hundreds of Premiership games as a player. He knew how fast it was, what it sounded like, what the banter was like. He also had the instant respect of the players because once a player, always a player, even if you've decided to join the dark side.

But ex-players turned refs don't get an easy ride for long. Eventually, players won't care less if the bloke in charge appeared a hundred times for Saracens or Munster or whoever, they'll just want them to do a good job.

Still, ex-players becoming refs in rugby is far more likely than ex-players becoming refs in football simply because of the money involved. If you've been earning a hundred grand a week as a footballer, you're not going to start doing

During the matches played behind closed doors in the 2021 Six Nations, dinner the nights before the games were somewhat different than usual. Here, Paul Adams, the Welsh referee manager, hosts the team of officials with a Deliveroo and Peroni before the Wales v. Ireland game.

Juno and Beau walking me to work before to my 100th game between NZ and Wales in Cardiff.

Joël Jutge presents me a framed World Rugby refereeing shirt to celebrate my 100th game.

Brian MacNeice, Christophe Ridley, Karl Dickson and me two hours before kick-off between France and South Africa in Marseille in November 2022. The calm before the storm.

Presenting Tappe Henning the Referee of the Year award in Monaco a week after France v. South Africa in November 2022. (© Dave Rogers-World Rugby/Getty Images)

Richard Hill, Jason Leonard and Lawrence Dallaglio join me to commemorate my 100th cap at Twickenham before retiring to the Sun Inn at Richmond for a few more celebratory drinks.

Juno and Beau at the RFU celebration for my 100th cap. A classy touch from Bill Sweeney by bringing my family, friends and colleagues into one room to mark my refereeing milestone.

Polly and the kids join me on the steps of Twickenham Stadium to celebrate my 100th cap.

Lyn Jones and me in my changing room after the Scotland and Russia match during the RWC 2019.

Eddie Jones, the coach, Kingsley Jones, the captain and David 'Lardy' Emery were all part of the 2017 the annual Forest v. Barnes charity match in aid of Breast Cancer Now at Lydney RFC.

Polly and her school mates, Ferne Gardner, Kelly Clarke, Gemma Bond and Jayne Sargent, making sure the annual charity match is another roaring success.

I may not ever get to hold a trophy aloft, but in 2019 during the World Rugby Awards evening, I did manage to get my hands on the Webb Ellis trophy for a few moments.

An hour before kick off with Siya Kolisi and Sam Cane. (© Julian Finney-World Rugby/Getty Images)

Preparing for my operation at St Barts

Me, Polly and the kids moments after the final whistle of the RWC Final.

Thanks to the lobbying of IRMO, all the match officials received RWC caps in recognition of being selected. We were presented ours at the Eiffel Tour.

a very stressful job that only pays you a hundred grand a year, at most. And it's not just the money: can you imagine the grief they'd get from the fans? It doesn't even bear thinking about.

In contrast, while people like Glen Jackson and Karl Dickson had great playing careers, they wouldn't have earned enough to retire on in their thirties. So even though they took big pay cuts to become referees – the starting salary for a ref in England until recently was not a lot of money given the scrutiny they're under and the abuse they get – it still made some kind of sense. Although I'm sure plenty of people have asked Glen and Karl, 'Why didn't you just get a job, one where you don't get screamed and shouted at?'

Former Gloucester prop Nick Wood also took the plunge and became a referee. He ran touch for me a few times, the irony being that I was the only ref to send him off in almost 300 professional games.

I red-carded Nick just seventy-three seconds into a game between Gloucester and Saracens in 2013, which was the second-fastest sending-off in Premiership history. Apparently, he'd been told that if he wanted to play for England, he needed to show more aggression. So he stamped on Jacques Burger's head, opening it up like a tin of beans. I didn't really have much choice but to send Nick off and he got an eight-week ban. He never did play for England.

In October 2022, in my final season, Nick was running touch when I refereed Newcastle v. Saracens at Kingston Park. That day, I had to send off Sarries prop Mako

Vunipola for a dangerous clearout. The incident triggered a melee, with a bunch of Newcastle players pinning Mako to the floor and giving him a telling-off. Mako's teammate Owen Farrell was incensed and screamed at me, 'They can't do that! He knows he's done wrong!' But after the game, Nick said to me, 'I'm pretty certain Owen was the first person to pin me to the floor when I stamped on Burger's head.' When I looked at the footage, he was exactly right!

If we want more ex-players to become referees – and more referees full stop – they need to know they're going to be looked after properly. As it stands, too few are convinced that would be the case.

When I chatted to Delon Armitage after he played in my charity match, he said, 'I get that your job is hard, what I don't understand is why you do it?' And when I recently asked Saracens' Jackson Wray, who has just retired, and former England flanker Matt Kvesic, who is in the twilight of his career, if they'd consider becoming a ref, they both laughed at me. They couldn't get their heads around why anyone would want to put themselves and their families through so much hassle for so little money. I couldn't really argue.

18

Hospitality

In 2009, a decision was made to use British and Irish refs on the Lions tour, which had never happened before. I was scheduled to referee the Lions v. Free State Cheetahs in Bloemfontein and run touch in three other games, including the one against the Sharks in Durban.

Like anyone into their rugby in the UK or Ireland, I'd grown up a huge Lions fan, so to be involved in a tour of South Africa was the stuff of dreams.

The officials stayed in the same hotels as the Lions, so I spent a few evenings drinking with the management, including head coach Ian McGeechan, forwards coach Warren Gatland and defence coach Shaun Edwards.

They were all very sociable, including Edwards, even though I found him slightly terrifying. The first time I had a proper drink with them was in Bloemfontein. Us officials were already in the hotel bar when they all filed in, and the wine really started flowing after that. It wasn't a case of bribery or corruption, Edwards just wanted to see how pissed they could get the young referee. They did a pretty good job, and I felt distinctly average the next day.

After the game in Bloemfontein, which the Lions won by a whisker, I joined both teams in what appeared to be the only nightclub in town, and it was great to see that famous Lions camaraderie up close. They were still a proper touring team back then, playing the game hard and having a few beers with their opposite number afterwards.

There used to be far more post-match ceremonies in rugby, where players and coaches would mix with officials, administrators and sometimes even owners. As a result, I got to know a lot of players and coaches quite well.

I remember reffing the Ospreys and being out in Swansea, with their coaches Sean Holley and Jon Humphreys, until 3 a.m. Then there was a Bledisloe Cup game in Dunedin, when I spent hours in the hotel bar with All Blacks scrummaging coach Mike Cron. He would have taught me plenty that evening.

When I refereed in Samoa a couple of years after the tsunami, my host for the week was Peter Fatialofa, who played in two World Cups in the 1990s. He took me on what he called a 'cup of tea tour', which was a bar crawl of all his favourite bars and restaurants across the country. By the time we got back to the capital Apia, where the game was taking place, I could barely speak, while Peter was just getting going. Mercifully, the game was a couple of days later.

In Fiji in 2022, Glen Jackson, the former player and referee, and now Fiji's assistant coach, arranged for me to go on a boat trip around some of the country's smaller islands. Whenever I'm in New Zealand, I'll visit a vineyard just outside Queenstown, which is owned by the former referee Lindsay McLachlan. And before Scotland played the United States in Houston in 2018, one of their referees, who also worked for NASA, gave me a guided tour of Mission Control, the room where engineers worked to land astronauts from Apollo 11 on the moon.

I was invited to lots of fascinating places and have photo albums full of snaps from all sorts of weird and wonderful occasions, because rugby folk often have interesting jobs and broad hinterlands, and love showing off their countries.

You had to go some to beat French hospitality, which was always top-notch. One of my first games in France was a Pro D2 (second division) game at La Rochelle, the 2023 European champions who were then on the way up. It was my first French trip and so my referee coach Brian Campsall, who spoke good French and was popular over there, came to hold my hand. Pre-match, there was a big function involving club dignitaries, and Brian said to me, 'You always attend. Shake hands with the president, eat your lunch and take some wine, as a sign of respect.'

Thirty minutes until kick-off and I still hadn't finished my tarte Tatin and they were still doing speeches. I said to Campo, 'Shouldn't we go?' And he replied, 'Just wait till they've finished.' I was still checking players' studs on the pitch five minutes before the game started.

La Rochelle won the game – just as the home team almost always wins in France – before we all got back to feasting and drinking. In the bar, I was presented with a La Rochelle beret and made to neck a half-pint glass of beer. Like Campo said, I had to do it as a sign of respect.

When I returned to La Rochelle in 2022, this time to referee a Champions Cup game, the president remembered that previous visit, which I thought was amazing considering the club's meteoric rise since then.

The more experienced I became, the more I was sent to France to referee games that were expected to be tight affairs, partly because the locals would usually be quite upset if their team lost. When Toulouse hosted Ulster in the 2022 Champions Cup, I sent off one of their players after ten minutes and they ended up losing. Afterwards, security had to escort me through the car park, just so I could have a bite to eat. The players and coaches thought it was hilarious. Former All Black Jerome Kaino, who was on the Toulouse coaching staff, said to me, 'Why the hell do you do this?' I replied, 'I ask myself that a lot.'

Occasionally, I misjudged the situation and went out for a few drinks when I should have got in my car and driven straight back to my hotel.

In 2018, I refereed an all-French Champions Cup quarter-final between Clermont and Racing 92. French sides always looked after us well – someone would pick us up from the airport, and we'd be taken out for dinner the night before

– and our host in Clermont was the former France fly-half and club legend Jean-Pierre Romeu, who looked more like a prop and didn't speak a word of English but was lovely all the same.

Racing were trailing by a point when Dan Carter came off the bench, jinked through the Clermont defence and set up Marc Andreu for a try. Everyone in the ground seemed to think it was a forward pass, but after looking at loads of replays on the big screen (they love a big-screen replay in France, because it puts extra pressure on the officials), I didn't think it was clear enough and decided the try should stand. The Clermont players, coaching staff and fans went mental. And they went even more mental when they lost.

My team and I had made the decision to duck straight out, until Jean-Pierre wandered over to us and said in French, 'I am the chief of this town, you'll come to my bar.' By 'my bar', he meant a massive beer tent in the stadium car park, jam-packed with angry Clermont fans. As soon as we walked in, I knew I'd got it wrong. It was their territory, we were moving into it, and I knew people weren't going to be okay with it. Clermont rarely lost at home, and they needed someone to blame.

We were sitting at the only table, nervously sipping pastis, when I noticed that other people had clocked us. Soon, we were surrounded, and things were getting quite aggressive. I thought people were calling us 'ducks', as in *canards*, and it was only later that I found that they were actually calling us *connards*, which means 'arseholes' or 'pricks' or 'bastards'. Take your pick.

Things got even spicier when a camera crew arrived on the scene. The assistant ref, Tom Foley, was pushing the camera away, the crew were jostling him, and Jean-Pierre was up in arms because this was meant to be his manor and he was ashamed that the locals were treating us in such a shabby way. We did manage to escape unharmed, but that was definitely one of those occasions we should have settled for a small bottle of wine from the minibar.

When I first started officiating in the Six Nations, the tournament's pre-match hospitality could be quite lavish.

In 2006, I ran touch for Italy v. Scotland, and I wasn't sure what to expect because no one had bothered telling me. As it turned out, I landed in Rome on the Friday and we went straight out for a seven-course fish dinner, with as much wine as we wanted. (Or not: Alain Rolland was the ref, and he doesn't drink, so I decided to stick to a couple of glasses.)

As I've already mentioned, French pre-match hospitality was always bang on. And in England, the RFU's head of refs would take the match officials and their partners out for a beautiful dinner at the Petersham Hotel in Richmond.

The pre-match tradition took a while to make its way down to the southern hemisphere where instead of eating dinner in a lovely restaurant on the Friday evening, I'd be sitting on my own in a pub eating curry and chips. (To be fair, the ex-refs who have come into management positions have tried to up their game in recent years, because they were always quite embarrassed about their own countries' lack of pre-match hospitality.)

Whenever France played Italy, the hospitality would be ridiculous, because neither of them wanted to be outdone. I'd finish a game, pop back to my hotel, get dressed up, and then be whisked off to a thirteenth-century château or some old Roman venue next to the Colosseum. All the men would be in black tie and all the women in ball gowns, and there would be about twelve courses and fifteen different wines.

The other teams would put on a decent bash in their stadiums, although COVID-19 was pretty bleak for us officials. The night before Wales–Ireland, six of us sat two metres apart in my hotel room, eating Deliveroo off our laps. Looking back, I'm not entirely sure that was legal. And after the game, I jumped straight in my car and drove home to London.

What I loved most about those post-match dinners was having a beer with the players and coaches, except for the time Scotland head coach Andy Robinson thought it was appropriate to tell me how shit I was in the middle of the meal. Andy was raising his voice and gesticulating, obviously grandstanding for the people around him, and I just had to sit there and smile. (Polly wasn't overly impressed and probably wanted to kick him in the nuts, but fortunately she thought better of it.)

Sometimes there would be a bit of an atmosphere if there'd been a controversial decision or two. And I didn't mind coaches having a quiet chat and telling me they disagreed with some of my decisions, which happened quite often, but I didn't really want the rest of the room to know about it. Plus, I'd worked with Andy when he was England head coach, refereed contact sessions and helped his team prepare, so I thought that was a little bit out of order.

After the post-match meal, there will be speeches. The president of each union, and maybe the captains, will thank everyone, although sometimes they accidentally on purpose forget about the referee. Or they might say, 'That was a difficult game today, wasn't it, Wayne?' You know you're in their bad books when they pull out that line. After the speeches, the match officials will be presented with a gift, usually a tie, sometimes something a bit different. I've got tons of Irish crystal, while the Welsh loved to give you something with the three feathers on, whether it be a boot bag, a wallet or a passport holder.

Some of the refs liked to keep a match ball as a souvenir. Someone would stick their head around our changing-room door and say, 'I can only find nine match balls, one of them has gone missing,' and the referee's bag would have a big rugby-ball-shaped bulge in it. You had to be careful about that sort of thing, otherwise you'd get a reputation, like the New Zealand cricket umpire Billy Bowden, who was criticised for openly souveniring match balls and stumps.

Not that I can stand in judgement of Billy, because that's exactly what I used to do in my student days. I'd be down in Hertfordshire or wherever, getting changed in the kit room, and I'd text a mate and say, 'There are some really nice shirts in here, what number do you want?' The following day, he might be walking around Norwich wearing the Letchworth hooker's shirt.

I have, of course, got older and more sensible (having a wife and kids will do that to you), but elite rugby has definitely got less and less social over the course of my refereeing career, which is a shame.

Post-match functions cost money, so teams have tended to avoid them since COVID. Also, players and officials nowadays are far less likely to risk having a few beers in public, mainly because of camera phones and social media.

My teammates have deleted an awful lot of pics from an awful lot of phones in bars across the world, while I was asleep in the corner. But for the last couple of years of my career, I was careful not to be snapped with a beer in my hand and a smile on my face after a game. And if I saw someone pointing a camera at me when I was out for dinner, I'd push the wine away. All it took was for someone to tip off the press – 'Wayne was drinking the night before the game, he clearly wasn't taking things seriously' – and that could have been very detrimental to my career.

Look at what happened to Jaco Peyper at the 2019 World Cup. Having refereed the quarter-final between Wales and France and sent off French lock Sébastien Vahaamahina for a deliberate elbow, a photo of Jaco making light of the incident with a group of Welsh fans appeared on social media and he was stood down for the semi-final between England and New Zealand. Jaco was just having a bit of fun, and even if it was clumsy and naive, to have people saying he should never referee again, and for World Rugby to come down so hard on him for it, was a massive overreaction.

I hope the fact that so many players and coaches have turned out for my annual charity game is evidence of a mutual respect, and I've always enjoyed sharing a beer with them. But I wouldn't say any of them count as mates.

You must have boundaries as a referee because, at some point, you might have to send them off. Or maybe you'll fail to send them off when you should have done, because you've developed too much of a friendship.

I was probably too chummy with players in my early days, especially on the sevens circuit when there was a big post-match function after every competition. (You can't fail to bond when there's a cheetah walking around the swimming pool, scaring the life out of everyone, as there once was after a tournament in South Africa.)

Even for the first few years of my international fifteens career, when I was the same age as some of the players, I'd often get drunk with them after a game, like the time I was invited to Tiger Tiger in Cardiff and ended up in a gay bar with Adam Jones and Ryan Jones. But as time went on, I drifted further away from the players.

I'd still have the odd lovely interaction, like the time I sinbinned Schalk Brits in his last game for Saracens, the 2018 Premiership final, and he gave me a big hug on the final whistle. Afterwards, I signed my yellow card and sent it to his dressing room. But I cut out the socialising with players almost completely, partly because I didn't want to be that sad middle-aged bloke out drinking with a bunch of blokes in their twenties and thirties, partly because I had a family at home, partly because I was worried about the media and public perception.

That's why my final European game, the 2023 Challenge Cup final between Toulon and Glasgow, was so special, because the officials all ended up in a Dublin bar with the Toulon team and management. If you can't have a booze-up in Dublin, where can you have a booze-up? Especially if it's your last ever game of club rugby.

I was chatting to Dan Biggar and England prop Kieran Brookes at the bar, as well as Toulon's director of rugby Pierre Mignoni and Richie Gray (the coach, rather than the Glasgow and Scotland lock), who I'd done some work with for World Rugby and is a consultant with Toulon. I also caught up with former ref Romain Poite, who is now on Toulon's coaching staff. I stayed until three or four in the morning, when gin and tonic was coming out of my ears. It was a nice reminder of how things used to be.

19

Rassie

My first gig of the 2022 autumn internationals was Wales v. New Zealand in Cardiff, which is exactly the sort of game every referee wants to be involved in. The fact that it was my 100th Test (I was only the second referee after Nigel Owens to reach the century) made it even more special.

The Welsh Rugby Union made a real effort. I was able to invite Polly and our two kids, and we all walked to the stadium together, hand in hand, me with my bag over my shoulder. When we got there, Polly took the kids upstairs for a burger and chips, while I went downstairs to speak to the front rows.

It was a great game of rugby, with New Zealand running in eight tries and winning 55–23, and afterwards I was invited into the All Blacks changing room, where their skipper Sam Whitelock presented me with a gift and said a few kind words. He reminded me that I had refereed him on his Test debut against Ireland in 2010, and while he didn't mention 2007, I felt the need to. It was nice that I was finally able to laugh about it with a bunch of All Blacks.

In the post-match function, the Wales captain Justin Tipuric said some nice words, before asking the debutants, Rio Dyer and Sam Costelow, to sing a song for the crowd. After they were done, WRU president Gerald Davies suddenly said, 'Are you gonna sing a song, Wayne?' So I gave them a rendition of 'Sloop John B', which was the current ref's song of choice, and got all the WRU alickadoos to join in.

I left Cardiff thinking there was no job I'd rather do than be a rugby referee and was really looking forward to the following weekend's game between Six Nations champions France and world champions South Africa in Marseille.

I've got some fantastic memories of Marseille. I refereed my first World Cup game there, New Zealand v. Italy, in 2007. There was also the Heineken Cup semi-final between Toulon and Munster in 2014, when Jonny Wilkinson kicked Toulon to victory, as well as the European Cup final between La Rochelle and Leinster in 2022, which La Rochelle narrowly won. It's an amazing city, the Stade Velodrome is a fine stadium, and I was delighted to be heading there again.

I also had lots of great memories of refereeing the Springboks and good relationships with some of their players.

The game had everything a rugby fan would want, including oodles of physicality, flair and controversy. The noise was deafening and the atmosphere febrile. It seemed like every time I blew my whistle, I was surrounded by irate players and there was pandemonium in the crowd.

After twelve minutes, I sent off Springboks flanker Pieter-Steph du Toit for dangerous play – French centre Jonathan Danty was in a vulnerable position on the floor and Du Toit took him out with his head. Eight minutes into the second half, I sent off French scrum-half and talisman Antoine Dupont for taking out an opponent in the air. Then, with ten minutes remaining, I yellow-carded South Africa's replacement flanker Deon Fourie for an offence at the maul. At the time, South Africa were leading by four points, but France scored a try and a penalty and ended up winning 30–26.

I knew there were big moments to discuss with my team, and I suspected I was going to be a headline because it was a very tight game with lots of tight decisions. I'd also sent off two blokes, and not just any old blokes: Du Toit and Dupont were the two most recent world players of the year.

Officials need immediate feedback, while the game is still fresh in the memory, so after a shower I grabbed a beer and sat down with my team for a hot debrief. And having reviewed the big decisions, we concluded that we'd got them right. Du Toit certainly couldn't have any complaints because he almost took Danty's head off, and Dupont knew he'd messed up because he was very apologetic before he trudged off.

While we decided to have a drink in the safety of the hotel bar, it certainly didn't feel like 2007, when I knew I was going to be in for a rough ride. But at some point after the game, Springboks head coach Rassie Erasmus started posting videos on social media of decisions he thought we'd got wrong. One was of Thomas Ramos apparently handing off Cheslin Kolbe with his forearm, another was of Willie le Roux being penalised for a forward pass.

Remarkably, Erasmus had only just returned to matchday activities after a two-month ban for a sixty-two-minute video he posted during the 2021 Lions tour of South Africa, in which he criticised the performance of Australian ref Nic Berry. As a result, Nic and his family were subjected to terrible abuse from South African fans, and his reputation as a referee was done a lot of harm. It didn't help that World Rugby took far too long to issue a strong statement defending Nic, because it's a political organisation which also has to worry about what individual rugby unions think.

Officials in any sport expect criticism, it's part of the job. But people need to understand that rugby is a chaotic game, played at tremendous speed, so referees are going to get things wrong. I got things wrong every single game I refereed, and I've got no qualms about admitting it. I didn't mean to, just as Owen Farrell or Harry Kane don't mean to miss penalty kicks. The pressure gets to them, they get their technique slightly wrong, it's just what happens.

Erasmus could have spoken to me and highlighted his concerns. I'd done that with coaches my entire career, either face to face or online. I want to learn, I want to get better, and I want coaches to understand why I made the decisions I did. For example, I could have explained to Erasmus that

Sipili Falatea's late try was allowed to stand because his knees didn't touch the ground. But Erasmus didn't give me that opportunity: he decided to review my decisions on social media instead. When people see the coach of the world champions publicly criticising a referee, they feel entitled to join in. The attitude seems to be, 'If he can do it, why can't I?' And because social media provides a cloak of anonymity, the criticism can soon curdle to ugly abuse.

I'm only on social media to promote the game, officiating and my charity match down in the Forest of Dean. I'm certainly never unpleasant to anyone. So when I started getting death threats, I thought to myself, *I understand that sport is important to people, but is this really happening over a game of rugby? What does this say about society as a whole?*

Then, beginning on Saturday evening, Polly started getting threats of sexual violence, which took it to a whole different level. When people started threatening the kids – one person said they were going to burn our house down with all of us in it, another said they were waiting outside the kids' school, another said they hoped they died of cancer – I felt like quitting on the spot, just as I'd felt like quitting after the World Cups in 2007 and 2011.

I was the most experienced referee in the history of international rugby, so I thought I was prepared for everything. But it's impossible to prepare for stuff like that. When it's just me getting abuse, I can compartmentalise it, tell myself it's not real. But when your family get sucked into any unpleasantness, it takes a heavy emotional toll and puts a strain on relationships.

When Polly and I first got together, she would take any criticism of me very personally. I'd be refereeing a big game and she'd be scrolling through social media, and if she spotted something nasty, she'd get upset and want to bite. She eventually learned not to drink and scroll, because that would make it even more tempting, even if it was an anonymous account with three followers.

We weren't together at the 2007 World Cup, but we were close, so she was quite cross about my treatment. Her mum had lost her battle with cancer a couple of weeks beforehand, so she couldn't understand why people were being so vile about something as unimportant as a game of rugby. She also took the view that I shouldn't do any media after that. Her attitude was, 'No one helped you, why would you help them?'

Over time, Polly became more comfortable with me talking to journalists, and less upset about people calling me names on social media. But the stuff after the 2011 World Cup, when Graham Henry suggested I'd been involved in match-fixing, and the 2013 Premiership final, when Dylan Hartley called me a cheat, it really got to her. And she'd still monitor what was being said about me on Twitter, Facebook, Instagram, etc. She'd say, 'Just because you're not on social media, that doesn't mean it doesn't exist. It influences what other people think, so you need to be switched on to it.'

Polly became very good at filtering out the constructive criticism from the outright abuse, like the time she told me to stop smiling before kick-off, because, in her words, it made me look like a 'smarmy twat'. She'd also see pictures of me in kebab shops, with a big drunk grin on my face and some fan's arm around me, and tell me to be more careful. I'm an optimist and think the best of people, but Polly's more savvy than me. She understands that not everyone's intentions are positive, and that a seemingly innocent picture could be twisted and used to harm my career.

What I didn't know was that Polly had been receiving messages for years. But because it was my policy not to read anything on social media, for the sake of my mental health, she'd been keeping them to herself. And the whole time, without her even realising, the cup had been getting fuller and fuller, until the Erasmus situation happened and it started overflowing.

Polly and I had some heavy conversations, during which she said, 'If something isn't done about this now, and the people in charge don't take steps to support referees and families, I'm going to release every single one of these messages and go really, really mad in public.' Polly wanted nothing to do with my rugby career, and while she didn't want to stick her head above the parapet and start screaming and shouting, she felt she didn't have any other choice.

Her anger and upset made me wonder why I was doing a job that was bringing misery and pain to my family. I also wondered if I had anything else to achieve in the game. I'd refereed 101 internationals, surely that was enough. Plus, I had another good job as a partner in a law firm, and they were keen for me to come back full time.

Polly and I did our best to keep our kids out of the loop, but they still would have known something was up. And it didn't help Polly's mood when a video I'd done, which included a scene of me and the kids with their school bags, was posted on the RFU's social media channels three days after the game.

I knew how to report threats to the police (there's not a lot they can do unless the culprits are in their jurisdiction, but I'll keep reporting them), and had friends and colleagues from the legal world who knew how to get in touch with the various social media channels and get them to act. But most people dealing with online abuse aren't as lucky as me.

Abuse of this kind has, sadly, been the norm in football for some time, but we need to do something before it also becomes the norm in rugby. Look at what happened to English ref Anthony Taylor after the 2023 Europa League football final between Roma and Sevilla: first, video emerged of Roma manager José Mourinho abusing Anthony and his team in the car park, before Anthony and his family, including children, were hounded by Roma fans at the airport and had to be saved by security. A bottle and a chair were even thrown at them.

That incident did make me wonder what might happen if I made a big decision that resulted in France being eliminated from the 2023 World Cup on home soil and I then had to get on the Métro or a flight back to Paris from Marseille.

People will say, 'Well, if refs did a better job, that sort of stuff wouldn't happen.' But that kind of behaviour is simply not acceptable, in any sport, at any level, whatever anyone thinks of the referee's performance. Can you imagine how that family feels about his refereeing career now? Can you imagine the pressure he's under to step away from it and do something else?

I can't prove that there was any direct connection between Mourinho's abuse and the behaviour of Roma fans, just as I can't prove there was any direct connection between Erasmus's words and the behaviour of South African fans, but you have to be aware as a coach or manager that if you slag off a referee in public, it might have a knock-on effect. And when it's so calculated, as in they've had time to think about what they're going to say and post on social media, it's even worse, because that makes it vindictive. They know the referee is going to be pilloried, and that his or her family might be pilloried as well, but they apparently don't care, which makes it unforgivable.

Unlike football, rugby union sells itself on the back of its values, which is why coaches who abuse their power need to be made an example of. Otherwise, things will only get worse.

Marius Jonker was the TMO for the entire Lions v. South Africa series in 2021, and he was given a torrid time. Marius, a South African, was appointed because the series took place in the middle of the COVID pandemic and the authorities couldn't fly anyone else in – although that didn't stop Lions head coach Warren Gatland from venting his fury. On top of that, South African journalists called Marius all sorts of names, and he and his family were sent a torrent of abuse.

I understand that COVID made things tricky, but there's no way Marius should have been put in that position. Also on that tour, Jaco Peyper had the unenviable task of refereeing the Lions v. South Africa A. That was another daft appointment, because Jaco had worked with a lot of those South African guys, and he was heavily criticised by both sets of coaches afterwards. It was like putting me in charge of an England game. (As an aside, I was given an early reminder of my lowly place in rugby's pecking order at the start of that tour: I got on the plane at Edinburgh and had to walk past all the Lions coaches and senior players in first class, then all the other players and support staff in business class, before arriving at my seat in economy. To be fair, they did lend me the Lions mascot to keep me company on the flight to Johannesburg.)

Ireland's Andrew Brace took some disgusting flack after a game between England and France in 2020, including people commenting on the obituary of his late father. And Kiwi Ben O'Keeffe has taken a barrage of nonsense. He showed me some of the horrendous messages he received after a game between Ireland and Australia in 2022, before sharing more abuse on his Instagram account following the 2023 Super Rugby final. One person sent him a message saying they knew where he lived and wanted to slit his throat.

What kind of people are we dealing with here? And is this really what rugby referees should be putting up with as a matter of course?

I should point out that the RFU were amazing after the France–South Africa game, with CEO Bill Sweeney and director of performance Conor O'Shea doing everything they could to support me and Polly, who they contacted personally. But it was still a shitty couple of weeks, and we referees decided we needed to take things into our own hands.

We'd been chatting about starting up an international rugby officials' association (called International Rugby Match Officials) for a while, not just to ensure we have a voice in the decision-making process, laws and general shape of the game, but also to ensure we're protected by the rugby authorities. That doesn't just mean psychological support for us, it also means supporting our families.

Ironically, I'd already been appointed touch judge for South Africa v. Italy in Genoa the weekend after the France–South Africa game. To be fair, the skipper Siya Kolisi, who I've always had a lot of respect for, sought me out at the post-match function to discuss the previous week, but I got the impression that even he didn't grasp the seriousness of his coach's actions (Erasmus wasn't there because he'd been banned for two games).

Siya told me he was sorry about what had gone on, and I said to him, 'It's all very well being sorry, but you're one of the leaders of this team and you've got to hold people to account.' Siya replied, 'You have to understand the environment we're in. It's difficult.' I understood that, because it is a tricky conversation to have with a coach who's led your country to World Cup glory.

Having built some great relationships with Springbok players, from refereeing them in internationals or club games, their changing room was now a different environment. Before, it had always been pleasant and collaborative, but now it was frosty, and it felt like some of the senior players no longer trusted me. In fact, I know they didn't trust me, because one of their wives had posted money emojis under Erasmus's social media outburst, obviously implying I'd taken a bribe. A few of the coaches took time to come and speak with me, including their impressive scrum coach Daan Human, who I refereed loads of times when he was at Toulouse, but I felt his embarrassment.

That was difficult because it had taken me years to build up that trust, and when players don't trust you, it makes refereeing them a lot harder. Also, like I used to explain to the England players when I worked with them, if you decide as a team that a referee is against you, your mindset becomes, 'He's going to penalise us whatever we do, so we might as well carry on behaving badly.' A far more positive way to deal with things, however, is to work out ways to stop the referee from getting involved and having to make decisions.

English ref Matt Carley handled that Italy–South Africa game extremely well and looked after me a little bit. In the lead-up, he pulled me aside and said, 'You've looked after us enough, now it's our turn to look after you,' which was nice of him. After the game, which the Springboks won by a mile, we were due to go out for a few beers, which I wasn't too enthusiastic about. But Matt sought out somewhere quiet and we ended up in a small, dingy bar just down the road from our hotel, which was just about perfect.

Alas, we were on our third or fourth gin and tonic when a pissed South African staggered through the door, walked straight over and clamped his very large arm around my neck, while saying, 'You were so shit last week . . .' I wore it for a while, because it began quite jovial, but as the arm got tighter, eventually I snapped and said, 'You need to get your fucking arm off my neck and get the fuck out of here.'

I don't normally swear or get aggressive, and this bloke was quite taken aback. And it was the trigger for the TMO, who was a French guy approaching sixty, to remove his glasses and offer the bloke out. His exact words were, 'You think you're a big man? Come and have a fight with granddad outside.' I was sitting there thinking, *Oh my goodness, this has taken a turn for the worse.* He didn't take granddad up on his challenge and was ushered from the premises, thank God. Who knows what the headlines would have been. Perhaps, WAYNE BARNES STANDS IDLY BY AS ELDERLY COLLEAGUE BEATEN TO A PULP.

Polly and I were meant to go to Monaco the next day because I'd agreed to present the referee of the year gong at the World Rugby Annual Awards, but Polly pulled out because she hated rugby and everything to do with it. I took a train on my own, and it was a rather bleak journey. I didn't enjoy that evening much, although I did have a wry smile when it was announced that referee of the year was a South African.

I was also due to be presented to the crowd at half-time of England v. South Africa at Twickenham, to commemorate refereeing 100 Tests, but I called RFU CEO Bill Sweeney and told him I didn't want to do it.

It would have been a nice way to say thank you to Polly and the kids for all their sacrifices but I didn't want to put them in a situation where they heard a horrible comment about their dad or husband from a disgruntled South African fan. It was just the wrong game at the wrong time, and Bill, who I have so much time for, understood, as did everyone else.

On the Tuesday, Bill arranged for a little get-together at Twickenham, with the family, some colleagues and various characters who had helped me along the way. World Cup winners Jason Leonard, Lawrence Dallaglio and Richard Hill were also there, and that was my chance to say thank you to everyone. That summed up the game of rugby for me, referees and players sharing a few beers and plenty of stories after all those years.

The following weekend, I was back in the saddle for a Premiership game between Harlequins and Gloucester. It was a classic match-up I'd been watching since I was a kid, and it was walkable from my house, so the perfect game at the perfect time. And a couple of weeks after that, I was over in Clermont for their Champions Cup game against South Africa's Stormers. I wouldn't say the Erasmus affair was suddenly a distant memory, but being a rugby referee at least made sense again.

20

Skippers

Over the course of my career, I dealt with many good captains – and some absolute terrors. There are some – Ireland fly-half Johnny Sexton springs immediately to mind – who shout and scream for eighty minutes – 'He was offside! Why did you give that? Why didn't you give that?' – and some referees will be swayed by that kind of confrontational approach. But I'm far more susceptible to captains who at least try to be reasonable. Nice blokes, in other words.

I had a lot of time for former Australia captain David Pocock, who would always come and find me after a game for a chat. That wasn't him trying to butter me up – he was just a polite, respectful chap. But I'm sure I gave Pocock a few fifty–fifty decisions off the back of it. Former Ireland captain Paul O'Connell wasn't a shouter either, he just knew the game inside out and occasionally asked a probing question. Wales's Sam Warburton was the same, someone who just oozed integrity.

Former Toulouse and France skipper Thierry Dusautoir didn't say much at all, which meant that when he did say something, I took notice. In a game between Toulouse and Montpellier, Montpellier did a blindside move, Dusautoir missed a tackle, and they scored in the corner. I wasn't going to refer it to TMO until Dusautoir approached me and said he'd been obstructed at the scrum. If that had been almost anyone else, I'd have fobbed him off. But because Dusautoir had never tried to pull the wool over my eyes before, I said we'd take a look at it. As it turned out, he had been held and we chalked off the try. (Although I did get flak about it in the media, with some journalists accusing me of setting a dangerous precedent. To be fair, they were probably right.)

Towards the end of my final season, I refereed Scarlets v. Clermont in the Challenge Cup quarter-finals. Scarlets' captain was Wales hooker Ken Owens, who all the referees get on well with because he's a decent bloke. Whenever I'd refereed him for Wales, we'd shared a couple of pints of Guinness after the game. He'd always be at the same end of the bar in the President's Lounge of the Principality Stadium, which he called 'Ken's Corner', and we'd chat about all sorts.

During the Scarlets–Clermont game, a driving maul collapsed, and I thought, *I've got to bin someone.* Ken was the most obvious culprit because he was hanging off the bottom of the maul, but there was another possible culprit on the other side. So I thought, albeit subconsciously, *I don't really want to sinbin Ken, because he's a decent guy and the captain.* So I sinbinned the guy on the other side, Scarlets' number five, instead.

This poor second row said to me, 'That's a bit harsh, isn't it?' and I waved him off. Meanwhile, Ken's given me a cheeky smile and a wink.

A good referee will keep telling himself, *Just referee what's in front of you.* Because if you don't, you'll make emotional decisions instead of the best ones. But some captains don't seem to appreciate that referees are human, so emotional decisions will inevitably slip through the net every now and again.

If you scream and shout at a referee all day, you're not going to get the rub of the green, those fifty–fifty calls are not going to go in your favour. And I would sometimes think, when a player was mouthing off at me, *Mate, honestly, in a minute I'm going to penalise you and I'll smile as I do it.*

The same goes for players who say the opposition has done something untoward and when I look at it on the screen, it's clear that they haven't. Those players lose credibility and the time when they do have a point, a ref may not be willing to listen.

I'm aware that there will be people reading this and thinking, *That's not being human, that's just being easily swayable.* But if you want humans making some decisions, instead of machines making all of them, you've got to take stuff like that into account.

One reason Sexton is so strident is that he knows his law, so when he's saying, 'They can't do that,' he's probably right. But Sexton will keep shouting at a referee even after they've explained their decision. That's counter-productive, because it's not respectful. I always said to players, 'You speak to me the way you expect me to speak to you.' And when a player screamed at me, I said, 'I guarantee I won't scream at you like that, so don't do it to me.'

If you try to tell your wife or husband what to do, over and over again, the chances are they'll do the opposite. Actually, it's more like a relationship with your kids. If your kids are playing up around the house all day, and then they ask you for an ice cream, you'll tell them not to be so ridiculous. Or if they keep crying wolf, you'll end up not believing them.

England's Owen Farrell has got a reputation for being a bit too mouthy, but I always got on well with him, as I did with most England players, probably because I trained with them and didn't referee them that much in club games. Of course, there was that run-in with Dylan Hartley, but that was the one and only time.

Wales fly-half Dan Biggar had a love/hate relationship with most referees, despite the fact that one of his best mates is the Welsh referee Ben Whitehouse, who he's known since school. Ben must have told Biggar all about the stresses and strains of refereeing, but he's one of the most difficult players to officiate. If he doesn't trust a referee, he can be a nightmare.

After Wales played France in 2021, when they were denied a Grand Slam by two late French tries, Biggar chased referee Luke Pearce off the pitch, while effing and jeffing at him. I was the TMO, and I was saying to Luke and his touch judges, 'You need to stay together and get off the pitch as quick as you can,' because I knew what a volatile character Biggar was and was worried.

For some reason, I always got on well with him. He'd always come over for a chat during the warm-up and I'd have a beer with him afterwards. Most people will tell you he's a lovely bloke off the pitch, which just goes to show what competition does to people. The minute they cross that white line, they can turn from Dr Jekyll to Mr Hyde.

I'm sure there were plenty of eyebrows raised when Biggar was made captain of Wales for the 2022 Six Nations, because the best captains are those who ask well-timed questions politely and sow seeds of doubt in a referee's mind, not constantly badger them and cause them to dig their heels in.

When the TMO came in, clever captains learned to get their ammunition in early. They'd say stuff like, 'Darnesy, just remember he dropped his height in the tackle,' or 'Just be careful he wasn't pushed,' and that would be in my mind before I'd even started looking at the replays. And while I was looking at the replays, there would be a chance I was thinking, *He might have a point there . . .*

One captain people imagine must have got up refs' noses was All Blacks great Richie McCaw, because he had been widely accused of being a serial cheat.

McCaw played 148 Tests and was only sinbinned three times (I showed him his last yellow card, against Argentina at the 2015 World Cup, when he tripped Juan Martín Fernández Lobbe), but he was constantly accused of pushing the boundaries of legality, and not just by people on Twitter. The list of opposition coaches and players who called him a cheat was long, and included France number eight Imanol Harinordoquy, who claimed that McCaw played the whole of the 2011 World Cup final offside.

But I always thought the argument that McCaw was allowed to get away with murder was lazy. If you look at the stats, McCaw gave away more penalties than most international back rows, so the argument that referees weren't keeping a proper eye on him doesn't stand up. Neither does the argument that he intimidated referees, because he hardly ever spoke.

A more charitable view is that McCaw knew the law book inside out, was very good at judging how a referee would interpret the breakdown, and knew what he could get away with. Laws have edges, which are blurred. For example, what is a side entry? It's essentially a gate, but gates can move, depending on how players shift around, and McCaw was more aware of that than most.

McCaw was also brilliant at getting over the ball. So many times when New Zealand were under pressure, he'd turn it over and truck up the field. He reminded me of Martin Johnson in that his attitude was, 'Give it to me, I'll sort this out.' So, I'm sorry to disappoint you, but Richie McCaw was fine by me. A good skipper is a wily skipper, and McCaw was as wily as they come.

21

Coaches

Before most games, coaches would send me clips of things to look out for, usually to do with the scrum. So before the 2023 Premiership semi-final between Sale and Leicester, Sale's scrum coach sent me clips of Leicester tighthead Dan Cole allegedly collapsing scrums, and Leicester's scrum coach sent me clips of Sale loosehead Bevan Rodd allegedly collapsing scrums.

I listened, nodded and smiled, and while I never take a coach's word at face value, those clips did help me understand their main concerns. I needed to make sure I knew what Cole and Rodd looked like in strong and weak positions. And I could say to the teams, 'This is what I think will help ...' It might be scrummaging a bit higher, or taking their time at each stage of the formation sequence, or making sure they bind when I say bind.

When it comes to the scrum, it can be lots of different things. Thankfully, I had Roachy telling me exactly what to look out for. But that doesn't mean I always knew what was happening.

I always hear people saying, 'Refs haven't got a clue what's going on in the scrum' but that's unfair and doesn't take into account the time we spend working with scrum experts. I always try to make an educated decision, not guess as it is often suggested. I have got it wrong because it's easy to see the finished picture, i.e. the tighthead prop lying flat on his stomach, and automatically penalise him. But there are lots of other reasons why he might have ended up there, the loosehead dropping his shoulders below his hips for example. And sometimes you just cannot see everything.

If I was refereeing Australia v. New Zealand, New Zealand would usually send me examples of Wallaby flanker Michael Hooper infringing at the breakdown. If they had a point, I could then say to Australia, 'Just so you know, New Zealand have asked me to keep an eye on making sure Michael Hooper comes off the ball.' If I can convince teams not to offend before they've taken to the pitch, I've done a big part of my job. I don't want to be a policeman, I want to ensure continuity and momentum, and make the game more entertaining.

I've been helping the England team prepare for tournaments since the Martin Johnson regime. And I refereed all their training matches before the 2015 World Cup, including the game that clinched Sam Burgess's place in the squad.

Sam had been one of the best players in Australian rugby league, a bloke who'd won man of the match in the 2014 NRL final, so there was a real excitement around him. In the minus column, he'd only been in rugby union for a season. So one of my jobs was to try to upskill him, explain the laws, so he didn't keep getting penalised. The problem was, when I first chatted to him at Bath, he was playing six, then when I chatted to him in the England camp, he was playing twelve. I said to him, 'We'll get you there, but I'm not quite sure where we need to get you,' because six and twelve are different roles with different requirements.

When England chose Sam ahead of Northampton centre Luther Burrell, it was controversial, but he was excellent in that final training game, so it made sense to me. And he played okay in the World Cup, despite some people blaming him for England's failure to reach the quarter-finals. As he said to me when I had a beer with him in Australia recently, 'As I remember it, we were fucking winning when I went off with ten minutes to go.' I thought that was a fair point.

The next time I saw England's head coach Stuart Lancaster, after that final training session, was at Buckingham Palace, where they held a reception after the quarter-finals. He and his skipper Chris Robshaw looked shellshocked, and I thought, *Oh my goodness, I've been through the wringer as a referee, but I can't even imagine what it must be like for them, their side having failed to reach the knockout stages of a home World Cup.*

I worked with Stuart right up until the end of my career, and he was always unbelievably kind with his time, as I know he's been with lots of coaches all over the world. He'd help me prepare for certain games, but I also spoke to him about the World Cup aftermath. He was deeply wounded by the flak he took, and the fact his family got dragged into it made it so much worse.

He did great things at Leinster, who won one Champions Cup and reached three more finals while he was on the coaching staff, and I think he'll have more success at Racing 92 in France, who he joined in 2023. I reckon he's still got an itch to scratch in international rugby, and I'd love for it to be one of the great redemption stories because he's one of the nicest men in rugby.

My overriding impression of Eddie Jones as England head coach was that he craved information. I'd meet with him every couple of months, usually at the start and end of a campaign, and he'd want to know what referees were seeing and thinking that he might not have picked up on.

After he lost forwards coach Steve Borthwick (in 2020) and defence coach John Mitchell (in 2021), I got the impression their replacements weren't able to give their views in such a forthright way. I was at a training session down in Bristol when Eddie called a halt to proceedings and berated his coaches – 'Why is this session not good enough? Why aren't you good enough?' – and it felt like an old-school headmaster giving a group of supply teachers a dressing-down. I think it made everyone feel quite uncomfortable.

At the same time, I sensed the players liked Eddie. He was obviously a hard taskmaster, but there was also fun and mischievousness. And Eddie was far too smart to be unpleasant to me. I'm not suggesting he knew he'd coach Australia again one day, but that's how things panned out, and I'm refereeing the Wallabies at the 2023 World Cup. By the time you read this, you'll know how that went.

Readers might be surprised to learn that, until recently, referees had one-on-one meetings with coaches before internationals. I'd have half an hour or so with one head coach, before having half an hour or so with the other one. That was their chance to highlight concerns about the opposition, as well as telling me what they were planning to do and asking if they'd get away with it.

The obvious problem with refs and head coaches meeting before a game is that it's open to manipulation and bullying. And since the Rassie situation, the authorities have stopped refs and head coaches meeting face to face, although the ref can have a call with the forwards coach.

But I found those meetings very helpful, for a couple of reasons. First, if a team was planning to adopt a certain tactical ploy, I'd be able to say, 'No, you'll get penalised for that,' or, 'Yeah, that's within the laws.' Either way, I'd know to look out for it. I'd also want to know about any special plays, so I wouldn't get in the way. For example, they might have a move from the back of a lineout, which involves passing back inside to the winger, and I'm not going to be very popular if it hits me instead.

You were more likely to get a smoother game by chatting things over with the coaches. But not always. You might remember the Six Nations game between England and Italy in 2017, when the Italians wouldn't compete for the ball after a tackle, meaning rucks weren't formed and there was no offside line. As a result, the Italians were able to stand among the England backline and prevent the ball from being passed. Italy head coach Conor O'Shea had run the ploy past Romain Poite before the game, and Romain had told him that while it wouldn't go down very well, it wasn't against the laws, so they could do it.

Romain was right, it didn't go down very well, but there was nothing he could do to prevent a terrible spectacle (at one point, England flanker James Haskell asked him to clarify what he wanted to see for a ruck to be formed, and Romain replied, 'I'm not a coach, I'm a referee'). Conor's reasoning was that Italy, who couldn't buy a win in the Six Nations, needed to do everything within the laws to compete, however cynical.

Some coaches – Rassie Erasmus being an extreme example – want to win at all costs. If they need to use the media to protect their position, they'll do that. So if a key decision cost their team three points, they will tell the press they lost because of the ref. But not all of them are like that.

I don't think I've ever heard Exeter's director of rugby Rob Baxter make a comment on the refereeing in a post-match presser. So when he phoned either me or my boss on the Monday or Tuesday, he had more credibility than someone who was constantly bashing refs in public, or indeed someone who would send me or my boss forty or fifty clips of supposed mistakes I made (always when they'd lost).

I didn't mind them saying to me before a match, 'This is what we're trying to do, this is what we're trying to achieve, is this or that legal?' But some would say to me, 'The other team does this, they also do that, so you've got to do this, you've got to do that.' I'd think, *Really? I've been doing this job a long time now, I'm pretty good at it, and you're trying to tell me how to do it?*

Before the 2023 Premiership semi-final between Sale and Leicester, one of the Leicester coaches took it upon himself to tell me how to referee things. The first opportunity I got to penalise Leicester for doing the thing this coach had told me to stop the other team from doing, I took it.

Sale boss Steve Diamond warmed to me towards the end of my career, but there was a period when he seemed to think I was the scum of the earth. He'd glare at me whenever I walked into their changing room, which I was convinced was his way of trying to intimidate me and make me uncomfortable. And in 2012, he got a lengthy ban for verbally abusing me after a game between Sale and London Irish (I'd given a last-minute penalty and Sale had lost by two points).

Steve came storming on to the pitch and started screaming and swearing at me, and at the post-match press conference, he said I had arrived late for the game (I was just in another room), didn't understand the scrum laws and was out of shape. I thought, *Anything else, Steve?* And while I'd probably had a few too many turkey dinners at Christmas, an ex-hooker calling me fat was a bit rich.

In my final season, I refereed at Llanelli and one of the coaches started screaming at one of my touch judges because she had missed a trip. The video referee picked up the trip no more than ten seconds later, and the coach came over and apologised for giving her a hard time. But I still felt the need to say to him, 'I guarantee you I won't scream and shout at your players every time they miss a kick or drop a ball, so please don't shout at us when we miss something.'

Then you'd get the coaches who would literally laugh at you as you walked off the pitch, often while clapping sarcastically. Northampton's assistant coach Dorian West did that to me after the 2013 Premiership final, when I sent off Dylan Hartley. Because I thought people should be held to account for their actions, the next time I refereed Northampton, I said to Dorian, 'Are you going to clap me today as I'm walking off?' He replied, 'Oh, that was just in the heat of the moment.' I thought, *I would like to see how you'd react if I made decisions in the heat of the moment.*

Some coaches would be nice and polite to me before kick-off but wouldn't speak to me afterwards, whatever the result. That told me that their pre-match friendliness wasn't entirely genuine. But someone like former Ireland lock Donnacha Ryan, who's now an assistant coach at La Rochelle, would always come and have a beer with the refereeing team after a game.

I refereed Donnacha as a player for the best part of two decades, and after Leinster beat Racing Metro in the 2018 Champions Cup final in Bilbao, he must have been in our changing room for half an hour.

Then there was the time Russia head coach Lyn Jones came into my changing room with a bottle of vodka after a World Cup game against Scotland in 2019. I'd known Lyn for years, so I said to him, 'Lyn, what have you got to celebrate? Your team has just lost by sixty points.' He replied, 'Yeah, but we're at a World Cup . . .'

I'm sure people will say I was being played, but I'd rather think that some players and coaches just appreciated my efforts and enjoyed my company. I'm not naive, I realise that people try to curry favour whatever job you do. But when you're a referee, genuine relationships take years to develop, so I was pretty good at spotting when someone was being fake.

22

Balance

Juggling two careers made it almost impossible to get the work–family balance right, especially when my two children appeared on the scene.

Not long after my son was born, I was due to run touch for Ireland v France in the 2017 Six Nations. The night before, I put my phone on silent because I needed to get a good night's sleep. And when I woke up the following morning, I had a load of missed calls and messages from Polly, telling me I needed to ring home as soon as possible, because our son had been taken seriously ill and was in hospital.

I jumped on the first plane out of Dublin, and when I arrived at the hospital, the poor little fella was lying there in his nappy, attached to a heart-rate monitor and a machine that was helping him breathe. That's when I realised that I needed to start thinking less about my career and more about my family. Yes, I could have done with a good night's sleep before the game, but making myself uncontactable meant I wasn't there for my wife and son when they needed me.

As I got older, my coping strategies became more advanced, so unless something really controversial happened, I wouldn't bring my work home. Polly will tell you that I never really displayed any negative or positive emotions connected to a game of rugby for the whole time we have been married.

Polly says I crave peace and calm, which on the face of it is pretty odd for someone who's a referee and a barrister. But I need that peace and calm to be able to operate in an ordered way. Emotion clouds logic and decision-making ability, which isn't great if you're a referee or a lawyer.

I'm not one of those referees who mopes around the house for days after a bad game, making everyone else's life a misery, and I'm not one of those referees who gets really nervous and goes into their shell before a big game.

I'd take the kids out on the day of a Test, while Polly always talks about the Heineken Cup final between Toulouse and Biarritz in 2010, when she had a wardrobe meltdown and insisted we go shopping for a new outfit in a sweltering hot Paris. A few hours before kick-off, I was standing outside a dressing room in H & M, when I probably should have had my feet up. But I was able to do that without it affecting my mood because I'd prepared so well.

The fact I was able to remain so unflustered before big games made Polly wonder if I was a psychopath. I'm pretty sure I'm not a psychopath, but it's fair to say that my mind works slightly differently to most people, even other referees. As a result, Polly worries that I'll have a meltdown at some point, because I've been holding too many emotions in for so long.

But for too many years, I didn't say no nearly enough because I disliked confrontation and worried it would be held against me. I didn't question why I needed to be in New Zealand or South Africa for that extra week or two, because I thought that maybe someone else – someone keener and more amenable – would take my place next time around and do a better job.

I allowed too many meetings that were meant to last an hour go on for longer. I expected Polly to drop everything if something happened to the kids, even though she had a career of her own. And remember, I wasn't just a referee, I also had my legal work. That meant working until midnight most days, including Sundays, because that was the only way I could fit it in around my family, my friends and my rugby.

Elite sportspeople spend an awful lot of time away from home, but if you're a Premiership rugby player, you'll have a fixture list at the start of the season. If you play for England, you know what the schedule will be for the Six Nations, summer tour and autumn internationals. But a referee will only find out on the Monday where they're officiating on the weekend and whether the game is on a Friday, Saturday or Sunday. Sometimes, I would find out I was going away on international duty just two weeks beforehand, and it might be a week in South Africa or three weeks in New Zealand.

Imagine having a couple of young kids and your partner suddenly announces they're off to Australia in five days' time, and they won't be back for three weeks. Imagine all the reorganising you would have to do, the meetings with friends and family you'd have to cancel, the awkward conversations you'd need to have with your boss. That randomness can put a big strain on the family, and partly explains why there are so many broken relationships in the world of rugby refereeing. Without wanting to come over all 'woe is me', that's also why I think we're undervalued.

I wish I'd made better decisions earlier in my career, but I also wish my bosses had better understood that rugby referees, while tremendously privileged to be doing the job they chose to do, have lives outside the game.

Back when I started refereeing, referees tended to be older and their children more grown-up. But referees nowadays are often in their thirties, with younger kids and more independent partners. They're having to juggle being active parents with being pulled from pillar to post by rugby. Polly is every bit as successful in her career as I am, if not more so, but for too long there was an expectation that my job took priority. Certainly, my managers seemed to think that I should simply do as I was told – namely be wherever they wanted me to be for as long as I was needed – and any effect on Polly was never a consideration. This makes me wince, thinking about it now, because it's a horribly old-fashioned, sexist way of viewing relationships.

If I ever ended up in management, I'd hope I'd be able to say to people, 'We don't expect you to be away for twelve weeks this year. We're going to make sure you have plenty of time with your family and friends. And don't worry, it's not going to damage your career prospects in any way.' That way, maybe someone will match or even surpass my record of five World Cups.

As difficult as it was at times, I tried to be less selfish towards the end of my career. If there was a meeting that was scheduled to finish at 8.30 a.m. and I needed to drop the kids off at school, I'd leave the call at 8.30. It wouldn't matter how important the call was, I'd simply tell them I had to go. Or if Polly texted me in the middle of a match review to tell me that one of the kids was sick and needed picking up, we would discuss who had the most important day. And if it was Polly, I'd say to the lads, 'Sorry, this will have to wait.'

They're the kinds of conversations that most modern couples have, or at least should do if they both have nine-to-five jobs. But when you work in sport, whether as an athlete, a coach, an official or a journalist, there are always going to be times when you're away for long stretches and your partner is left at home holding the fort. And it's not as if Polly's employers gave her ten weeks off while I was in Japan for the 2019 World Cup, she had to carry on working full time while looking after the kids, including ferrying them to and from school and making sure they carried on with all their activities at the weekend.

Despite all that, I know Polly wasn't looking forward to me retiring from being a referee, because she'd never known me as anything else. People kept saying to her, 'You'll get him back soon,' which really pissed her off because it inferred that I was only coming back because rugby was done with me. She was also worried about me being at home a lot, because she'd got so used to doing exactly what she wanted, whenever she wanted (kids permitting, obviously).

Polly said to me one day, 'Have you considered how it's going to feel when you retire? Because there's a strong possibility that you're going to fall off a psychological cliff.' I thought I'd be fine because I was retiring on my terms. But it's still early days, so who knows how I'm going to adapt to a new life without weekly club games, long trips away and major Test matches.

Maybe those holes will be more difficult to fill than I imagined. And it's not just the big holes, it's also the mundane little ones, right down to the fastidious way I packed my bag every week. I had the same Tupperware box for twenty years, covered in club badges from all over the country, the same manky old towel, the same boots, the same whistle, the same coin. But even if I do struggle with the transition, I'm sure Polly will just be relieved that she'll finally be able to look at her direct messages on social media without wincing.

23

The Final Whistle

People sometimes ask me if I'm able to appreciate the quality of play if I'm refereeing a particularly good game, to which the answer is always yes, absolutely. One of the great things about being a referee, in any sport, is that you've got the best view in the house of some of the world's finest athletes.

I once read about a football referee who played an advantage and gave a fist pump after the team scored a spectacular goal from it. I would never go that far – you'd never see me high-fiving a player after a length-of-the-field try – but I was always very aware when I was in the middle of something special.

Examples would be the Premiership final between Saracens and Exeter in 2019, when Exeter came out all guns blazing and scored three tries to two in the first half an hour, before Saracens ended up winning 37–34. That was one of the tastiest finals I refereed, a bona fide humdinger with incredible levels of athleticism and skill.

In terms of internationals, two games involving Ireland stick out. Their 2023 Six Nations encounter against France, which had pretty much everything, from Damian Penaud's stunning counter-attacking try to James Lowe's acrobatic and controversial score in the corner, which took ages for me and the TMO to award.

Then there was Ireland's win against the All Blacks in Wellington in 2022, a week after their first ever victory on New Zealand soil. Ireland scored three tries and were almost faultless in the first half, before the All Blacks roared back with three tries in twenty minutes after the break. When you're part of something like that, it's very difficult to stop yourself from smiling.

Sometimes, I would see a moment of sublime skill – a spectacular touchdown in the corner or a player slithering through the tiniest of gaps – and think, *I have no idea how he's just done that.* Or I'd cringe at a sickening collision or a defender being steam-rollered. During my final regular- season Premiership game between Bristol and Gloucester, Bristol centre Semi Radradra got the ball and ran straight over the top of Gloucester fly-half Adam Hastings. I felt so sorry for Hastings that I wanted to stop the game and see if he was all right.

I never got blasé about refereeing. To the very end, I'd look around the ground while the anthems were being played and think, *Jeez, this is a pretty special way to watch a game. What a privilege.*

One of my last games before the 2023 World Cup was a Bledisloe Cup clash at the Melbourne Cricket Ground.

Standing in the middle, just about to blow my whistle, I was suddenly hit by the enormity of it: 84,000 people gathered to watch a game of rugby – and hoping I didn't ruin their evening. But once I'd blown my whistle, I was able to appreciate the incredible athleticism on display. If I didn't gasp at a seemingly impossible offload or sidestep, I wouldn't be human. And, as I hope I've made clear, we refs are human.

I was never quite sure when I was going to retire, and the result of that uncertainty was that I cared less and less as my career went on, which made me a better referee. I refer back to what Eddie Jones told me about players and refs being at their best at the start and end of their careers, because they don't think or worry as much and let their personalities shine through.

I seriously considered hanging my boots up after 2015, because I thought it would be nice to finish with a World Cup in my own backyard. But I enjoyed that tournament so much that I decided to carry on.

I definitely thought I was going to walk away after the 2019 World Cup. The *Guardian*'s Rob Kitson jumped the gun on that one. We were chatting away, and he asked whether I'd be reffing in the Premiership next season. I said something along the lines of, 'I don't know. I'll sit down with Polly after the World Cup and decide.'

The following evening, I was on way home from an appearance on TV when I got a call from the RFU's head of comms. She said, 'The bosses are really pissed off you told the *Guardian* you're retiring before them.' I replied, 'What? I've not announced I'm retiring!' But it was a lovely couple of weeks because people kept coming up and congratulating me for my contribution to the game. It was like getting a sneak preview of my obituary.

Even when England pulled out that amazing performance against New Zealand to reach the final, which ruled me out of the running, I thought, *Well, you can't hang around for four years on the off chance you'll do the final next time around.* But COVID allowed me to take a nice break from the game (although it wasn't great for the bank balance), and after being picked to referee a couple of games on the 2021 Lions tour of South Africa, I thought, *Well, the next World Cup is only two years away, I might as well hold on.*

As a referee, you need to know the technical stuff. But as time goes on, and you get more of a handle on the law book (as much as a rugby referee can ever get a handle on the law book), refereeing becomes more of an art form.

Early in my career, I was quite confrontational, even though I hated confrontation away from rugby. I thought the way to deal with angry, disagreeable people was to get in their faces and shout at them, but as time went on, and I became more comfortable in my own skin, I realised good, effective refereeing was far more subtle. It was about things like knowing when to smile, when to get involved, when to keep your distance and turn a deaf ear.

But those kinds of things only become part of a referee's armoury if you don't listen to too many people or fret about what anyone thinks. And they only became second nature for me after that tricky middle period of my career, when I was still worried about the politics and being selected for the big games. That meant scrambling to keep up to date with every law tweak and refereeing new directives too harshly, because I thought it would please my bosses, rather than refereeing how I thought the game should be refereed.

It's ironic that most referees are at their best at the point when they retire. Yes, the criticism and controversy can grind you down, but if you could beam me into Ellis Park for a game between the Springboks and the All Blacks, before beaming me back home on the final whistle, I'd carry on doing it. I'm only forty-four, so certainly physically able to keep ploughing on for a few more years.

It's the not knowing where you're going to be from month to month, all those flights, all those strange hotels, all that time away from loved ones, that eventually make you want to stop.

I saw a lot of referees come and go over two decades, and I was the last of my generation still standing. The blokes I started out with had become administrators, people like Joël Jutge, Tony Spreadbury, Bryce Lawrence and Craig Joubert, who were all match officials at the 2007 World Cup.

Towards the end of my career, I was speaking to the selectors more than my teammates, because they're the people I shared so many great times with during my formative years as a referee. That was a strange position to be in; I was suddenly the elder statesman, still wanting to perform well but not caring too much about the consequences, whereas most of my teammates were in the fearless early stages of their career or in that tricky middle period.

I spent a lot of time over the last seven or eight years of my career coaching younger refs, guys like Karl Dickson, Christophe Ridley, Tom Foley and Ian Tempest. I never thought, *Maybe I shouldn't give up my secrets, because one day they'll want to be refereeing the same big games as me.*

Older refs did the same for me when I was coming through the ranks, but there wasn't the same camaraderie as there is now. Back then, I was at a Q & A with four or five other refs and one of them, a senior international ref, was asked if we were all in competition with each other. He replied, 'Yes, most definitely. We're all after the big games.'

I liked and admired this bloke, but I was taken aback by his response. Yes, I wanted to be refereeing the big games, but I never viewed it in terms of being in competition with anyone else.

When I started reffing at international level, there were lots of big personalities, some of whom, rather than being helpful, seemed to be glad if other people made mistakes. I even heard about people deliberately missing foul play while running touch to make the ref look bad. Some of these guys are now in management roles, and I still hear about them slagging off fellow referees via text or email.

But I don't see that kind of behaviour among the group of international refs we have now (although I hope that's not me being naive and they were all in a WhatsApp group without me). For the most part, they have each other's backs and want each other to do well.

I'm looking forward to fading into the background and watching these young guys take the lead. And, unlike more pessimistic observers, I don't think they'll be officiating a game that's almost impossible to referee. My hope is that rugby's authorities become less fixated on the small things, and getting everything right, and start to think more about an overarching philosophy. Phil Davies, the ex-Wales international and Namibia head coach, is now World Rugby's director of rugby and has started those conversations. I hope he's the force for change I believe he can be.

If I wasn't just in charge but also had a magic wand, my first wish would be for rugby to stop with all the negativity. You get people slamming refs for sending players off for dangerous play, when everyone wants fewer concussions. You get broadcasters showing multiple replays of players getting smacked on the head. Players with early onset dementia who tell their story get accused of endangering the future of the game. There's constant talk about the financial implications for the game if legal challenges from injured players come thick and fast. Add in all the famous old clubs like Wasps and London Irish going into administration and it's a pretty gloomy picture. Sometimes I think, *I know this is all very important stuff, but can't we talk about the positive aspects of rugby for a change?*

I sit on World Rugby committees and see first-hand how much they're investing in trying to reduce head injuries but, for whatever reason, they are reluctant to publicise what they're up to. For example, Premiership players now wear gumshields that gather head-impact data. That's revolutionary stuff, something that no other sport is doing.

Where I do think rugby needs to make strides is in getting people to understand the potential risks of rugby when they start playing it at pro level. You'll never be able to make rugby completely safe, and it's the physical side of it that attracts so many people to the game in the first place, but people need to know the risks.

When rugby gets it right – and it still gets it right more than it gets it wrong – it's an amazing game. It can teach you so much, whether you're a kid playing touch or operating at the elite level. You learn to look after your mates, on and off the pitch. It instils resilience and teaches you the importance of discipline, whether it's turning up on time so you don't let anyone down or not punching the opponent who keeps kicking you in the shins. You learn empathy and tolerance and all sorts of people skills, especially if, like me, you've got a screw loose and decide to become a referee.

Rugby is one of the most social pursuits in the world. When I watch my children play at Teddington RFC, which is just around the corner from me, there are thirty kids in every age group, each with six or seven coaches. And after training, people stick around for a beer and a chat.

I've never stopped making friends through the game, from the time I first turned out for Bream RFC at the age of six or seven. Those lads I played rugby with at university – Ox, Bruno, Toon, Lurch, Byker, Crack, Candle and Uncle – are still close friends now, and we've never fallen out, even when one of them (I still don't know who) defecated in my bath at the 2007 World Cup.

When we stage our charity game at Lydney RFC, 3,000 people come to watch. The Debbie Broderick Memorial Cup is in its tenth year and is named for Polly's mum, who passed away from breast cancer. Sadly, Deb never got to see Polly and me together as a couple, despite laying the groundwork, many years ago – when Polly was ten and I was fifteen.

Don't worry, it's less creepy that it sounds. I was head boy at Whitecross School, which was no mean achievement for someone whose brother was one of the biggest maniacs to pass through its gates. One of my head-boy duties was to show prospective students and their parents around the school, and, one open day, I was given Polly and her mum.

At the end of the tour, Deb turned to Polly and said, 'You're going to marry him.' Polly replied, 'Don't be silly, I'm not going to marry anyone called Wayne.' To which Deb said, 'He'll have to change his name to William if he wants to be a barrister anyway, but don't let that get in your way.'

Lydney is a small town, so most youngsters went to the same pub, and I stayed in touch with Polly after I left Whitecross. When I was home from university, we'd see each other at Christmas and New Year's Eve in the only bar that stayed open past 11 p.m. She likes to remind me that

I asked her out for a coffee when she was seventeen, and she replied, 'Where do you think you're from? We don't do coffee in Lydney.'

We didn't see each other for a few years, but Deb kept her up to speed with my refereeing career. If there was an article about me in the *Forest Gazette*, she'd cut it out and send it to Polly, with a note that read, 'Get rid of Rich and go out with Wayne.'

Then one day I bumped into Polly at London Bridge. I was at a rugby meeting and she was out for a curry with some workmates, so I made sure not to mention coffee and asked her out for a few drinks instead.

When Polly and I got married in 2013, not that long after Deb had passed away, we asked guests to donate to Breast Cancer Now instead of buying us gifts. And afterwards a friend of mine who coached at Bream suggested we organise a charity rugby match.

The original plan was for Bream to play my old university mates, but I thought we needed some razzmatazz. So I asked some pros to come along, and two recently retired England players, scrum-half Shaun Perry and hooker Lee Mears, said yes.

The game now takes place between a Wayne Barnes XV and a Forest of Dean XV, and we've had some proper legends turn out for my team, including Jamie Roberts, Ken Owens, Geordan Murphy, Phil Vickery, Ugo Monye, Lewis Moody, Delon Armitage, Dave Attwood and Matt Banahan. Then, of course, there's me. In case you're wondering, yes, I am still a non-tackling back row.

We've also been coached by Warren Gatland, Eddie Jones, Mike Ford and George Skivington. When I asked Eddie to come down, not only did he turn up an hour before kick-off, but he also had photos taken in the changing rooms, gave a speech, did a bit of coaching, and stuck around for photos and a quite a few glasses of wine afterwards. He's had a lot of bad press, but he showed he was a true rugby man that day and the people of Lydney adore him.

At the time of writing, I've still got a World Cup in France to referee. Until my involvement was confirmed in writing, I wasn't certain I would be going. I was in decent form, but you're always slightly worried. I think my apprehension was mainly down to the fact that it was the last chance I'd get to do it and I wanted it so badly.

I even said to Polly, 'If they don't pick me, I'll be retired from refereeing with immediate effect, so we'll need a plan.' Polly being more combative than me, she replied, 'If that happens, you're not going quietly. I'm gonna get you interviews with X, Y and Z, and I'm going to kick up a huge fuss on social media.' I was thinking more about what we'd do together over the summer.

I hope I don't get mentioned too much because that will mean I've done okay. I'm not doing the opening game between France and New Zealand, which was probably a wise decision, given what happened in 2007, although if they meet again in the final, I'll obviously want to be there.

But if France don't win the World Cup, I foresee controversy, whoever's in charge, at whatever stage.

The last time the World Cup was played there in 2007, not much was expected of them. This time they've got a very good team, so anything less than World Cup glory will be a disappointment. Whoever referees them in the knockout stages will be under a lot of pressure. And a controversial penalty decision or sending-off could prove incendiary.

We've been asking World Rugby for months now, 'What are you going to do if there's a major fuck-up in a big game?' We'll just have to keep our fingers crossed that they stick up for us.

To be fair to World Rugby, under Alan Gilpin, the CEO, they have made it clear they won't be commenting on refereeing decisions during the tournament. But we'll see, because they have contradicted themselves by approving Whistle Watch for the tournament, so our high-profile decisions will be dissected by Nigel under the World Rugby banner. That blows my mind and has disaster written all over it.

Having blown my whistle for the last time, I'll probably take a break from rugby. I was in discussions with the RFU about taking up some kind of official coaching role, but while I would like to keep my hand in coaching some of the new guys on an ad hoc basis, I might also be tempted to work in another sport for a couple of years, because I don't want to become jaundiced towards rugby.

I'll be able to commit more time to my legal activities, which will come as a relief to my partners. I work for a big law firm called Squire Patton Boggs, specialising in white-collar crime and government investigations, but that role also means I spend a lot of time conducting reviews and investigations for sporting bodies. It's not quite the same buzz as refereeing Ireland v. France in the Six Nations, but it can certainly be interesting. And I don't have to work on weekends, which is the main thing.

Maybe in a few years' time I'll return to rugby and try to make some changes from within. Refereeing at World Rugby needs a total overhaul, a clear philosophy and a coaching structure, so that all its match officials know what's expected of them. And it needs to protect officials and their families better. Alan Gilpin, the CEO, continues to support and back referees, because he understands the pressures we are under. If he remains in charge, I think things could change for the better, but I worry that World Rugby will keep kicking that stuff down the road, until something terrible happens.

My advice to any youngsters thinking about becoming a ref? First, carry on playing for as long as possible because you're a long time retired, and you'll make so many lifelong friends on the field and in the bar afterwards. Once you start refereeing, you will still be able to have a few beers after a game, but you'll spend quite a lot of time flying solo and make a fair few people grumpy.

You'll be shouted at by players on the pitch and fans on the touchline, and some days you will wonder why you bothered giving up your Sunday for no more than a burger and a couple of pints. Want a tip? The next time someone starts mouthing off at you, hand them your whistle. I've done that a fair few times, and they always give you a look that says, *God no, you carry on . . .*

However, you'll also be the beneficiary of so much kindness because, while there are some wallies out there, most rugby people respect referees, understand what a challenging job it is and are grateful that there are people willing to do it. One thing's for sure, there wouldn't be much rugby without us.

Refereeing might not be as much fun as playing, but there's not much in it. And you'll still be on the stage after all your mates have hung up their boots. But if a youngster tells me they're thinking about refereeing as a career, I'm a bit more cautious. People find out I was refereeing in the Premiership in my mid-twenties and assume it must have been easy. But it wasn't, and there aren't many who make it. And if you have a couple of bad seasons, you're out of a job.

That said, if you're a youngster who's suffered a career-ending injury or you haven't quite made the grade as a player, give it a go and see if you enjoy it. The lows can be very, very low, but the highs are almost impossible to imagine.

You'll never get to hold a trophy aloft or be lauded in the media (unless you're mates with Steve James!). But you will have a lot of laughs, visit some amazing places, meet some fantastic people and bank a lot of memories. And maybe you will end up appearing at a World Cup after all.

It's almost time for the full-time whistle. Just one last thing, in case you were wondering: having tried my hand at refereeing and lawyering, I won't be going into journalism or politics. There's only so much flak one man can take.

24

A Heart Stopping End

Training with Karl Dickson and Christophe Ridley is enough to give an old man a cardiac arrest. Karl only retired from playing a few years ago, Christophe is barely into his thirties. So when my heart rate started going through the roof during a running session in Paris, I wasn't overly concerned at first.

Maybe I hadn't slept well, maybe I hadn't eaten enough for breakfast, maybe I'd drunk too much coffee. Whatever it was, I thought my heart would go back to normal if I just took things a little bit easier. But fifteen minutes into what should have been a nice gentle jog, I looked at my watch and my heart rate was up at 230 beats per minute. My legs were like wet spaghetti, I couldn't fill my lungs. And I was refereeing the crucial pool game between Wales and Australia four days later.

To add some context, my resting heart rate is around 50 beats per minute. When I'm busting a gut during a game, it may reach 175, so 230 during a warm-up was, by anyone's standards, through the roof.

You might remember that I'd had ticker issues in the past. Back in 2009, I'd been diagnosed with atrial fibrillation and had an ablation operation. A few years after that, I went into tachycardia, which basically means my heart was racing and unable to regulate itself, and my cardiologist Richard Schilling had to reboot it. So naturally I wondered if the same thing was happening again. And while I wasn't scared, as in, 'Shit, I'm going to die', I did worry that my fifth and final World Cup might be over almost before it had started. I had already refereed a pool game between Ireland and Tonga, but that's not really how I wanted to sign off.

I rested on Friday morning and my heart calmed down. I didn't even bother telling Polly about it because I thought it had rectified itself. But the first thing she said when she arrived in Paris that afternoon and got a look at me was, 'You're not well. What's wrong?'

I travelled down to Lyon the following day, and my heart hadn't stopped racing by the Sunday, which was when the game was taking place. So now I was in a bit of a dilemma: if I told the bosses about my issue, my tournament – and refereeing career – would be over; but if I didn't tell the bosses and refereed the game, I was worried that I'd be miles off the pace. I didn't think I'd collapse or anything like that, I just thought I might let the players down.

My heart kept speeding up and slowing down all day Sunday, but I decided I was going to do the game. But when I looked at my watch during my warm-up, it was already running at 180 bpm. I crossed my fingers and hoped it would rectify itself before kick-off. Unfortunately, it didn't.

Three minutes into the game, Wales executed a move off a lineout and scrum-half Gareth Davies went flying over for a try. It was a start I could have done without, seeing as it required me to run about fifty metres. When I reached the try line, a few seconds after Gareth, I thought, 'Oh shit, I'm in trouble here . . .'

I limited my running as much as possible for the rest of the first half, which both teams made easier for me by giving loads of penalties away, but I knew I had to tell my fellow referees during the break. A camera crew was following us around for a documentary (more about that later), but once they'd got a bit of footage of us talking about our first-half performance (the consensus was that we'd done pretty well, ironically), I asked them to leave.

Once the camera crew had made themselves scarce, I said to my fellow refs – an all-English team of Luke Pearce, Christophe Ridley and TMO Tom Foley – 'Right, a bit of a problem, my heart has started racing, but it has happened before and I'm sure it will be fine.' A slight underplay you might say, but I didn't want to worry them. 'Luke, keep in mind that you might be taking over from me if it gets any worse. Meanwhile, I'll referee a bit more in between the two fifteen-metre lines to save my legs, so if you spot something blatant on the blind-side where you'd normally expect me to be, just call it.'

When I refereed Ireland versus France in the 2023 Six Nations, the ball was in play for forty-seven minutes. But that night in Lyon, the ball was in play for just thirty-one minutes. Tries and shots at goal slow the game down and there were three tries and eight penalty kicks that night. Still, had it been a tighter game, I'd have been in trouble.

Luckily, Wales hammered the Aussies 40–6, and I didn't have to make any match-defining decisions. And far from being disappointed with my performance, the selectors said it was as good as I'd ever refereed (they didn't even notice that Luke had bailed me out, making a decision when I was in the wrong position). Plus, I barely got a mention in the papers, which is always a good thing.

I didn't have a beer during the debrief in the changing room after the game, which was the first time that had ever happened. That was also the first time I'd ever answered the phone from the changing room immediately after the match; Polly rang and asked if I was okay, to which I replied, 'Not really.'

I woke up the following morning thinking my World Cup was probably over, which was a devastating feeling. I'd muddled through Wales–Australia, but it wouldn't have been fair on the teams to referee another game in that kind of condition. However, I thought I might still have one trump card up my sleeve: Richard Schilling, the guy who had done my ablation surgery back in 2009.

When I called to tell him what was going on, he replied saying he thought I'd looked fine. When I told him I hadn't felt fine, he told me to get hold of an Apple watch and send him an ECG reading. I was going to borrow one from somebody, until I found out that my readings would appear on their phone and they'd probably think I was dying. So after training on the Tuesday, during which I did as little as possible, I headed into Paris, bought an Apple watch and sent Richard my ECG reading. He replied saying my heart was in tachycardia again, but that he could see me in London the following day. He made it sound as if it was nothing more than a cold, which put my mind at rest.

As luck would have it, Wednesday was our day off, so I booked myself a 6 a.m. flight and was back in London before breakfast. I popped home and said a surprise hello to the kids, before heading to St Bartholomew's Hospital, which is just around the corner from the Old Bailey. When I walked past the Bailey, I thought to myself, 'That's my life now, because I'm not going to be a rugby referee for much longer.'

I shaved my chest at the request of the nurses and got all garbed up when Richard appeared with the anaesthetist. 'Here's the guy who's going to knock you out,' he said, casual as anything. 'Everything will be fine. I'll see you in a few hours.' The anaesthetist asked me what game I was meant to be refereeing next, and I replied, 'If I wake up again, it's Scotland versus Romania on Saturday.'

While I was out for the count, Richard restarted my heart, and when I saw him again, he told me it had all gone to plan. After I was discharged, we couldn't find a cab anywhere, so Polly and I jumped on the bus to Waterloo and then headed back home to Twickenham. This was probably not advisable after having been in an operating theatre a handful of hours before, but by this point I was desperate to see the kids before I had to rush back to Paris. I also spent the entirety of the train journey hiding my hospital wristband underneath my sweater in case any eagle-eyed rugby fans spotted me on the train and put two and two together.

The following morning, I dropped the kids off at school and went back to St Bart's for an ultrasound, to see if everything was working properly. Richard told me my left ventricle was still enlarged, that he might have to perform another ablation somewhere down the line, but that I'd be okay for the rest of the tournament.

A few people asked for a selfie on the Eurostar back to Paris, but I had to tell them I couldn't give them one because I wasn't meant to be in England.

When I got back to Paris, I decided not to tell the bosses what was going on because I thought they might panic, and they'd have had every right to stand me down. After all, if a player told their coach that they'd just had a heart operation under general anaesthetic, it's highly unlikely they'd let them play a game a few days later.

The following day, I travelled to Lille for the pool game between Scotland and Romania, hoping that the heart incident was a one-off. Richard had given me a special pill, so that if my heart did start racing during the game, I'd take it, my heart would calm down and I'd hopefully make it through to the final whistle.

I managed to conceal my shaven chest and the burn mark from the paddle that had been used to jump-start my heart from my fellow referees in the changing room – it was an Aussie and two Kiwis this time – and got lucky with another one-sided affair, Scotland trouncing Romania 84–0. I didn't even have to pop Richard's special pill.

To be honest, my misfiring heart was easier to deal with than some of the interesting management that was going on. We'd arrived in Paris a week before the opening game between France and New Zealand. We were due to be away for two months, so I'd been working my backside off to get everything done before leaving England, both in terms of legal work and family. And after the welcome dinner, I decided to go straight to bed rather than having a few drinks. My fellow referees were taking the piss out of me – 'Ooh, look at Wayne taking it all seriously' – but I was absolutely shattered, and we had training and one-on-one meetings with the selectors the following morning. It didn't sit well with me – I was normally leading the charge – but I was struggling to keep my eyes open and so it had to be done.

I was woken the following morning by a loud knocking on my door. It was Bryce Lawrence, a selector from New Zealand, wondering where the hell I was, because my one-on-one meeting was meant to have started five minutes earlier. When I checked my phone, I discovered my charger had a loose connection and my battery was dead, meaning my alarm hadn't gone off. As a result, I hadn't just missed my one-on-one meeting, I'd also missed our first training session of the tournament.

When I walked into the meeting room, looking extremely dishevelled, I launched straight into a grovelling apology – 'I'm really sorry, my phone didn't charge and my alarm didn't go off, but it still shouldn't have happened' – and Joël Jutge, the head selector said, 'We'll speak to you later.' I felt like a schoolboy being roughly dismissed by his headmaster.

Four or five hours later, there was a loud knocking on my door again. When I opened it, Bryce was standing there, with a quizzical look on his face. 'Are you taking the piss?' he said.

He reckoned they'd told me to come back at two o'clock, which is not how I remembered it, and now it was five minutes past. He'd actually done me a favour: having noticed I was late, he'd said he was popping out to the loo and come and got me. I owed him massively.

Joël looked very disappointed when I finally made it to the meeting. I explained what had happened all over again, promised that I'd check my phone's connection and set two alarms in future, but he informed me that I'd have to stand up in front of the entire match officials group and apologise for my behaviour. I said, 'I've already apologised to the people I needed to, which is you and the trainer. This is like being back at school.' But he wasn't for turning.

When I started apologising at the team meeting the following morning, I could hear sniggering throughout the room. Most of my fellow referees thought it was hilarious, but I thought the whole thing was pretty amateur.

But that wasn't all. During the one-on-one meeting, after the dressing down, Joël said, 'Wayne, you refereed well down in Australia and New Zealand. But people always say to me, "If you tell Wayne how to do something, he'll do it a different way." So I want you to listen more to the other referees.'

It was a ridiculous statement and one I didn't take well. I'd appeared in four World Cups before then, and had so much experience to draw on, but that made no difference. At that point, I decided that for the rest of the tournament, unless they asked me a direct question in meetings, I wouldn't get involved or stick my neck out. So, I sat in the corner saying nothing and making notes. I spent hours trying to help others over coffees or on walks around Paris, but not in team meetings. I was determined to *listen* more.

The strange thing was, Joël and I refereed in a similar way, so I could only conclude that there was a kind of weird power play going on. I suspected the boss thought I'd got a bit too big for my boots, whereas the truth was rather different. I'd always gone out of my way to help younger referees, and yes, I got more media attention than anyone else, but that happens when you've been on the scene for two decades. Yes, I spoke up if I didn't think something was right, but I thought I always did it in the proper way. I was certainly never undermining or confrontational.

I'd never felt like a shoo-in for the final – it was everyone else who seemed to think I was – but now I was starting to think there was some kind of conspiracy against me. They'd probably say they were just trying to keep me on my toes and stop me becoming complacent, but again, I thought it was pretty amateurish.

As was the whole TV documentary shambles. The production team who followed us around in the build up to, and throughout the World Cup filming for the *Whistleblower* documentary were first-class, really engaging and understanding (even when I kicked them out at half time of the game between Wales and Australia), but we still hadn't given them permission to use any of the footage they'd captured by the time we'd arrived in Paris. World Rugby told us we'd just have to take their word for it that they wouldn't stitch us up, but we told them that wasn't good enough. We wanted the ability to sign off the final edit and without that agreement, no one would be agreeing to participate in the documentary.

In the end, I asked some of my colleagues at Squire Patton Boggs to draft a contractual agreement between us and World Rugby to ensure we had the final say. It only got signed off by both parties two days before the opening game.

Whistleblowers, which you can watch via the RugbyPass website, is fantastically well-made documentary, although it's not the greatest advert for becoming a referee. I hoped it would focus a little more on the closeness and camaraderie of the group, but it's mainly about all the abuse we get and how hurtful it is to us and our families. I'm not sure anyone who's seen it will be doing a refereeing course any time soon.

On the bright side, at least the rugby authorities hadn't sprung any last-minute law changes on us (unlike previous World Cups). My first experience of the new bunker system, which was to be used at the 2023 RWC, was when I refereed the Bledisloe Cup game between Australia and New Zealand at the Melbourne Cricket Ground in July 2023 (83,000 people turned up to see the All Blacks hammer the Wallabies 38–7 that night). I also had the warm-up games to get to grips with the new foul play referral system. And all the referees were glad it was in place for the World Cup because it meant we wouldn't have to make any red card decisions; that would be left to those in the bunker. Though the on-field officials could technically decide to send off a player, we agreed as a group, prior to the World Cup, that unless someone committed some act of thuggery, we would leave it to the bunker, they had more angles and more time than the officials on the pitch

The one bone of contention was who was in the bunker. The TMOs weren't keen because they didn't think it tied in with their skillset, which was interacting with the referee live during the game, so the bosses decided to put two TMOs in the bunker but not name them, to save them from abuse if they had to make a contentious decision. But that was contentious in itself, because if people don't know who's in the bunker, how do they know if they're sufficiently qualified or even sufficiently impartial? As a result, they did end up having to tell the teams who was in the bunker, and amazingly no names have been leaked.

Except for heart scares and being told off for being naughty, my pool stage passed off without much drama. And my reward for staying under the radar on the field of play was the plum quarter-final between Ireland and New Zealand, which many people thought could have been the final.

I'd refereed the third Test between the sides in Wellington in 2022 and the intensity had been off the chart. There had also been plenty of niggle. But I wasn't just chuffed that I'd been given that game, I was also chuffed that they'd chosen to keep our team of English refs together. Christophe Ridley, Matt Carley and Tom Foley were three people I trusted and respected hugely, and I couldn't think of a better bunch to have around me if things got sticky.

As it turned out, there wasn't much controversy at the Stade de France. It was nip and tuck throughout, and some of the play was of the highest quality, and that last passage of play, when Ireland went through thirty-seven phases while desperately searching for the winning try, was about as stirring as rugby can get. I knew I'd been part of a very special game when I blew the final whistle, and the reaction of the players and coaches suggested that me and my team had done our job well. There was no grumbling from the Irish, just an acceptance that the All Blacks had been ever so slightly better on the day.

It was a breathtaking weekend of quarter-finals, which also included Argentina's upset of Wales, England's ding-dong victory over Fiji and South Africa's one-point win over France. The only major controversy was in that final game, when Springbok winger Cheslin Kolbe charged down a Thomas Ramos conversion attempt, which led to Kiwi ref Ben O'Keeffe getting terrible abuse.

The pool stage had mostly been gleeful for me – Ireland–Tonga in Nantes was a riot of noise and colour, as was Wales–Fiji in Bordeaux, while I'll never forget the Irish fans singing Zombie at the end of their game against Scotland – but I considered myself lucky that I didn't have to referee any of the host's games, particularly in the knockout stages. France has become quite a hostile place, rugby-wise, these past few years, presumably because they've had a winning team for the first time in a while, which comes with expectation. So when France went out, not only was the tournament poorer for it, I also knew that Ben was in for a rough ride.

Wherever he went for the rest of the tournament, people were giving him a load of shit, and I can imagine the abuse he got on social media too. He also refereed the semi-final between England and South Africa and got a hostile reception when he walked onto the pitch, there being a lot of French fans in the ground. That was sad to see, because Ben's a great referee and a good friend.

I also don't think I would have done anything different to Ben on that conversion decision. Even after watching multiple replays, I still couldn't tell if Kolbe had started his run too early or not. And anyway, how was he supposed to see it from where he was standing?

The Monday after the weekend before, Joël Jutge called me into his office and said, 'Wayne, we thought you were great. Congratulations, you're going to referee the final.'

'Unless England are in it,' I replied. The camera crew were filming that exchange, and Joël had to tell them that that conversation would not be making the final edit.

I'd been through this scenario before at the previous World Cup. And having been told that I'd be refereeing the final if England weren't in it, they played brilliantly to beat New Zealand in their semi-final in Yokohama.

South Africa had put everything on the line in beating France, and though they had been heavily criticised throughout the tournament, I suspected England had a decent game in them. They weren't going to play with width, like France, they were going to stick to a simple game-plan, be strong at the set-piece, tackle like demons, and hope that Owen Farrell had a good day with the boot.

Me and the rest of the English refs watched the semi-final in our team room at our hotel, and it soon became clear that the Springboks were shattered while England were massively up for the battle. And the longer the game went, the more my emotions got twisted.

I'd trained with England all summer, knew the players well and really wanted their head coach Steve Borthwick to be successful, after all the flak he'd taken. But when England led 15–6 with eleven minutes to go, courtesy of five Farrell goals, I started to think, 'Oh wow, I might have refereed my last game after all. I'll finish on 110. But there's not much I can do about it.'

Polly and the kids were coming over the following day, and I sent her a text saying, 'Looks like we're going to be drinking a lot of wine this week.' Then Springbok lock RG Snyman bundled over for a try, before a scrum penalty and Handre Pollard's winning kick.

I understood Ben's decision, but it was one of those decisions which I knew would split opinions. I think a lot of England fans were just frustrated that the game had been decided on something they didn't really understand. Lawrence Dallaglio brought a lot of heat on Ben by accusing him of winning South Africa the game on ITV, although he did ask me for Ben's number and did get in touch to apologise a few days later.

There were no high fives in the team room, despite the fact that we were heading to the final. Instead, it was a strange mixture of deflation and relief. I phoned Polly about half an hour later and the first thing she said to me was, 'It's a shame, isn't it.' 'What?' I replied. It turned out that she'd heard one of the kids having a nightmare with about five minutes to go, gone upstairs and missed the dramatic conclusion. As a result, she thought England had won.

The Thursday before the final, Polly and I took the kids to Euro Disney. I got some strange looks from South Africa and New Zealand fans, not just because they thought I should have been back in my hotel room preparing, but also because I was wearing Mickey Mouse ears and going on every single rollercoaster possible. But it was just the thing to take my mind off the game, as well as some of the interesting management that was still going on.

The assistant referees were sent home after the quarter finals, so I asked World Rugby if Christophe Ridley could be brought back out to run touch in the final; he'd done every major game I'd refereed over the previous two or three years and I wanted him to be part of my last one. But as expected, World Rugby's computer said no. Still, it was an all-English team for the final – me, Karl Dickson, Matt Carley and Tom Foley, with Luke Pearce as the reserve official. And we spent most of that week (except when I was strolling around Euro Disney) working out what the game was likely to look like: New Zealand would have parity in the scrum, because that had been one of their strengths throughout the tournament, so the biggest challenge would be the breakdown, because the All Blacks would want lightning quick ball and the Springboks would be desperate to slow things down.

There wasn't an official pre-final dinner, so the five of us organised to go to a local restaurant with our partners and kids, about a ten minute walk from the hotel. My kids were still wearing their Mickey Mouse ears, while I decided against it.

I got my hair cut on the morning of the game (far shorter than I wanted, but that's my fault for not paying enough attention in French classes at school), then returned to my hotel to reimagine the game a few more times.

What me and the team hadn't predicted was a player croc-rolling another and dropping his weight onto his knee as he did so, which is what All Blacks flanker Shannon Frizell did to Springboks hooker Bongi Mbonambi after just two minutes. That meant I was in the game far earlier than I hoped I would be, but at least it wasn't me who had to decide if it was a yellow or a red. If Frizell reappeared, fair enough. If he didn't, it was nothing to do with me. As it turned out, the officials in the bunker settled for a yellow.

Twenty-five minutes later, All Blacks skipper Sam Cane misjudged a tackle on Jesse Kriel, his shoulder making contact with the South African centre's head. I had no idea if it was a yellow or a red, and again I didn't give it much thought. But while Frizzell got away with a yellow, Cane's final was over.

Five minutes into the second half, Springboks captain Siya Kolisi became the third player to be sent to the sinbin, for a high tackle on Ardie Savea. Kolisi's yellow wasn't upgraded as the bunker officials decided there was mitigation as some of the force went through Savea's body and there was a change in dynamics in the tackle.

I understand the New Zealand fans' frustration. Neither player meant any harm, they just got their tackle technique slightly wrong. But one player remained on the field while the other one was gone.

Things could have got pretty hairy for me had we not had the bunker system doing most of the dirty work. It was two of those most passionate sets of rugby fans in the world, plus thousands of French and other nationalities, combining to make a deafening din, and I could barely hear myself speak.

The most controversial decision we had to make during the game was chalking off an Aaron Smith try. The TMO protocol said we could only go back two phases to look at technical offences, but I had missed a big knock on at a lineout three or four phases earlier. We'd discussed these types of situation as a group in the four years leading up to the final and during the tournament itself, we'd regularly say, 'Forget about the protocol, you can't have a World Cup final being decided on a technicality.' So as soon as I saw the knock on the big screen, I disallowed the try but awarded a penalty to New Zealand for a lineout offence by South Africa prior to the knock on. Beauden Barrett scored a couple of minutes later, which helped to take the sting out of the decision.

The All Blacks chucked everything they had at the Springboks in the final ten minutes and had a chance of victory when Kolbe knocked on deliberately and was sent to the bin, but Jordie Barrett's long-range kick drifted wide. A few minutes later, I blew my faithful old whistle for the very last time, and South Africa had won their fourth World Cup and second in a row.

Despite all the big decisions we had to make, I massively enjoyed my final game. It was a classic match-up – like 1995 all over again – in the magnificent Stade de France and I felt tremendously privileged to be involved. I had my team around me, I knew they had my back, and it was the best possible way to bow out.

As we waited for the presentation ceremony, I watched the fireworks with Polly and the kids on the touchline, while trying to find Richard Schilling and his daughter in the crowd. I'd sent them a couple of tickets as a gift, because if it weren't for him, I'd have watched the game from my living room in Twickenham.

There's a picture of me shaking Sam Cane's hand at the end of the match, and I thought that was classy of him, because I can't even imagine what must have been going through his mind. In fact, the whole All Blacks team were excellent, and second-row Sam Whitelock, who had also just appeared in his final international, even took the time to come and have a chat and ask me what I had planned next.

The most surprising conversation was with Rassie Erasmus, who finally apologised for what he'd said about me on social media. The apology was about a year too late, but I congratulated him and thanked him for it anyway. Then I went back to taking it all in and soaking it all up for one last time, grateful also that my heart had held up.

For the first time in my 111 games, I didn't do a post-match review in the changing room, we just sat there, beer in hand, and enjoyed each other's company for one last time. Back at the hotel, we joined friends and families, and reminisced into the early hours of Sunday morning.

The following day was the World Rugby awards at Opera Garnier, not just a chance for the players and coaches to be applauded, but a chance for all the refs to get together and say their goodbyes. Ireland's Andy Farrell was named coach of the year, Ardie Savea, the player of the year, and surprisingly South Africa only had one player in the World Rugby 'dream team', while New Zealand had four and Ireland and France five each.

That night was the first time I'd been made aware of all my stats: I was told I was the most-capped referee in history, with 111 Tests; I was also involved in ninety-three Tests as an assistant ref, with three more as TMO; I'd appeared in a record five World Cups and refereed a record twenty-seven World Cup matches; I was only the second Englishman to referee a final after Ed Morrison in 1995; I'd refereed a record twenty-six Six Nations games across seventeen Championships, as well as thirteen Rugby Championship matches. But I've never been one to bask in attention, so my fellow refs and I made our excuses and headed to the nearest pub.

It was time for one last post-match drink-up, almost thirty years after that fateful game between Bream Third XV versus Berry Hill Wappers, when someone had slipped me a fiver in the clubhouse, given me a tankard with 'Referee' engraved on it, and filled it to the brim with beer. And I'd thought to myself, *This could be the hobby for me . . .*

Epilogue: The Final Fall Out

It was only once the dust had settled that our decision to disallow that Aaron Smith try became an issue. World Rugby left me alone after the final because I'd retired, but poor old Tom got it in the neck. He had been told by the referee management immediately after the match that it had been the right decision to interject on the knock on, he had received a glowing exit interview and had been told that he would be officiating at the Six Nations, but a few weeks later he suddenly found himself dropped. Joël Jutge told him that he hadn't been up to scratch for the entire World Cup, which made no sense to me seeing as he was apparently good enough to be TMO in the final.

It transpired that World Rugby had been getting a load of grief from the Kiwis and rather than defend their man, they caved under pressure. As a result, Tom thought, 'After all the personal sacrifice I've given to do this job, if that's how I'm going to be treated, I'll retire.' That whole episode was so disappointing. Tom had been the victim of a political witch hunt and rugby had lost one of its best TMOs as a result, all because he'd wanted to do what was right and what we had all agreed we would do.

I copped a shed load of online abuse after the game, and sadly, so did Polly again. It was some comfort that World Rugby's Chief Communications Officer, Dom Rumbles, had been forward thinking and hired an AI company called Signify to monitor all the referees' social media accounts, identify trolls, and send the evidence to prosecutors. Some of Signify's stats were mind-blowing: three match officials were in the top ten most targeted individuals of the tournament, refs received 49 per cent of the total abuse sent during the tournament and I was the most trolled person in the entire World Cup, receiving a ■■■■ of all abuse sent to individuals. These are not stats we should be proud of.

Signify's sleuthing led to prosecutions across the globe, and I hope it sent out the message that abusing people online, even anonymously, has consequences. And when I say abusing people online, I don't mean shouting at me for sending off Sam Cane and not sending off Siya Kolisi (even though I didn't make either of those decisions), I mean threats of violence.

I certainly didn't miss any of the online abuse in my early days of retirement, and I didn't watch much rugby either. I only started tuning in again to see how my old referee mates were getting on, including Christophe Ridley, who did his first Six Nations in 2024, and performed very well.

I'm still living in Twickenham, so when England are playing at home, the refs will pay me a visit beforehand. And before South Africa played Wales at Twickenham a couple of weeks ago, my old mate Jaco Peyper, who now works with the Springboks, came over to my house for a couple of beers.

But hanging out with old refereeing friends hasn't made me want to dust off the old whistle. Even when I did start attending games again, including the 2024 Premiership and Champions Cup finals, which were both great spectacles, refereed by two excellent English referees, I never once thought I'd like to be out there in the middle of it all.

At the time of writing, I'm back working full-time for Squire Patton Boggs, which continues to be fascinating, and a role which means I am surrounded by so many talented young lawyers. I have also joined the board of the RFU, who should be applauded for widening the perspective of the Board by appointing an ex-professional referee for the first time, and I'm still involved with the International Rugby Match Officials association, who persuaded the organisers of RWC 2023 to give World Cup officials caps at the pre-tournament ceremony for the first time, so it's having an impact.

Some of the stranger offers I've had since hanging up the whistle include a white-collar boxing match against Richie McCaw. They offered to fly me and my family to New Zealand and put us all up for a week, but the idea of fighting one of the hardest rugby players in history on his own patch didn't really appeal, particularly as I'm a wimp. The New Zealand equivalent of *I'm a Celebrity,*

Get Me Out of Here asked if I'd be interested. Amanda, my agent, said to them, 'He's been ridiculed and abused by Kiwis for the last seventeen years, so he's clearly going to be made to eat and drink vomit fruit for three weeks solid. Make a sensible offer and we'll think about it.' They never replied.

Having given over my weekends to rugby for the best part of three decades, they're now mine again, to do with what I want. I'll never get all those birthday parties, weddings, funerals and lads' weekends that I missed back, but hopefully I won't miss many in the future. And hopefully Polly will adjust to having me around to support with the kids, having got used to running the show on her own.

I take the kids to football on a Friday evening, to cricket on a Saturday morning, we do 101 things on a Sunday, and I love every minute of it. I've even been able to plan a holiday this year for the first time ever. So come summer 2024, I'll be the bloke floating on a lilo, with a broad, contented smile on his face. Probably thinking, 'I'd do it all again in a heartbeat, but thank God I'm here now . . .'

Acknowledgements

In this book I talk about sliding door moments. Moments that change the course of your life, your career and your relationships. Those fundamental moments in my life were shaped and created by the people around me and without them I would not have been able to referee over one hundred test matches, become a partner in a massive law firm or write this book. To those people, I am eternally grateful. Many of them I mention within this book: Ashley Thomas, my teacher; Brian Stork and Wayne Cleaver, my pupil masters; Nigel Yates, Tony Spreadbury, Chris White and Brian Campsall, who shared their expertise in refereeing with me; Phil Keith-Roach and Stuart Lancaster, who have given me an insight into rugby that I would not have been able to find on my own.

But there are many others not mentioned within the main body of this book who have been as equally influential; far too many to name within the collection of stories, but who

I want to thank and acknowledge. Teachers such as Joy Johnson and Jackie Longton at Whitecross School, Peter Anthony at Monmouth School and Professor Ian Smith at UEA. The referee coaches who took me under their wing when I started off in Gloucestershire, Colin Edmonds, John Hackett and Andy Melrose to name a few. Mike Runswick, Mike Stott, Paul Storey and Dave Broadwell who welcomed a rather odd-looking law student into the ranks of the Norfolk and the Eastern Counties refereeing societies. Then as I climbed the ladders, Geraint Davies and his fantastic wife Mag, who not only coached me, but fed and watered me as I joined the National Panel of referees. Other top-class referees such as Greg Hinton, Sean Davey and Nick Williams always had an eye out for me as I progressed through the ranks, acting like a big brother at the early stage of my officiating career. Then the London Referees' Society who were so welcoming with their time and company when I arrived in the big smoke: Garry Fielder, Peter Crouch, Mark Powell, John Coates, Tim Miller and Gary Dibden.

Internationally, many people went the extra mile to improve me as referee, though it was not expected of them or within their job description, they would watch my matches, provide useful feedback and offer their own unique insight. Lyndon Bray, Andrew Cole and Michelle Lamoulie all helped make me better a referee.

During my time as a referee, so many individuals sacrificed time away from their families so they could support me and make my job easier. Assistant referees like the Benjamin

ACKNOWLEDGEMENTS

Button of officiating, Paul Dix, Robin Goodlife and Peter Allan, TMOs such as Stuart Terheege, Rowan Kitt, Geoff Warren and Graham Hughes. My current colleagues at the RFU have put so much time and effort into making me look good and perform better, that any success that I have had, would not have been possible without them. Matt Carley, Karl Dickson, Tom Foley, Luke Pearce and Christophe Ridley have literally carried me and my bags around the world over the last four years, and I am not able to thank them enough. Previous RFU professional referees such as JP Doyle, Dave Pearson, Rob Debney, Greg Garner and Andrew Small have all had my back on more than one occasion across the globe.

As someone who didn't love the physical side of our job and who by the end of my whistleblowing needed a lot of more than tape to hold my body together, I wouldn't have still been running around the field without the help of Alex Reid, Julia Church, Julie Tollit, Barney Kenny and Sam Parsons. You've worked miracles.

My body never did fail on me during any of the five hundred plus first-class games, but my heart took a few beats out of turn on more than one occasion during my career. Professor Richard Schilling not only got it back in rhythm, but he did so in such a humble and calm way, that it felt more like routine dental check-up than significant heart surgery. He was also there to put my mind at rest when I thought my career had ended prematurely in the middle of my final few games. Only Richard could make 'pop back to London and we will re-start your heart' sound like an attractive option. I will be forever grateful.

As a lawyer people continue to believe in me and, as explained within the book, I often wonder why. But my thanks to John Coffey at 3 Temple Gardens, David Williams at Fulcrum Chambers and all those who made me feel part of the team since joining Squire Patton Boggs in January 2022; Jonathan Jones, Steven Sampson and Jane Haxby, you took a punt on me and I hope to be able to pay it off over the coming years.

This book would never have taken place without the support, perseverance and odd bit of badgering from Amanda Heathcote. Amanda not only manages me, but she is also a great sounding board; she ensures that referees' voices are heard and she continues to be my number one advocate. She also takes a mean photo as you can see from one with me, Lawrence Dallagio, Jason Leonard and Richard Hill.

To Andreas at Little, Brown and Rory at the Blair Partnership, thank you for believing that people would want to read about the world of refereeing. Your advice and counsel throughout has made the process a lot less fretful than I had imagined, and your introduction to such an incredible writer in Ben Dirs was a masterstroke. I hope that you are as chuffed with the book as I am.

Ben, you have managed to bring my story to life with genuine humour but still with the insight and honesty I had hoped to give. To have a written record of the highs and lows of my career so well put together not only brought a smile to my face the first time I read it, but it will be something that I am able to look back on in years to come with great pride. Thank you.

ACKNOWLEDGEMENTS

To my university friends, as I said in the meat of the book, you are the best group of friends a bloke could ask for. As a referee, you are constantly pulling on a mask, never really able to be the real you. But when we get together, no matter where it is in the world, it is one of the few occasions I can be myself. Your time and advice have made the shit times, on and off the pitch, manageable and your piss taking always brings a smile to my face. I will always be glad I screwed up my A-levels and had to go through clearing and joined you at UEA.

Juno and Beau, you have sacrificed your dad being away for far too many weekends and on far too many international trips. I have missed you and thought about you on every single day of every single tour, and I cannot wait to make up for all of those sport matches and karate gradings that I have not been able to watch and all of those days I have not been able to hang out with you. I love you both very much.

Finally, to Polly. You have sacrificed more than anyone so that I have been able to achieve some of my personal goals. While I have been away most weekends and for decent chunks of the year, you've had to juggle being an amazing mum with two active children, along with holding down a hugely successful career of your own, while constantly helping others wherever possible, whether that be your friends, the professional women rugby players or someone who just wants your sage advice. No mean feat. You have also made me a better person. You have taught me to think differently. You make me laugh. You make me believe in myself. You hold me to account. You are my biggest fan.

I hate being away from you as I have no one to chat things through with. I cannot wait for this new chapter of our lives together. Thank you. I love you very much.

I am sure that there will be people that I have not thanked within this book but who have played a significant role in my careers. In the weeks and months to come I am sure I will be embarrassed and disappointed not to have mentioned them. But as I said above, I would not have been able to have become the person I am today without all of your time, advice and commitment. Thank you. I am truly grateful.

At a loss about the line out? Stumped by scrums?
Perplexed by the put in?

'Throw the Book' is a YouTube channel hosted by
international rugby union referee Wayne Barnes at his
kitchen table where he breaks it all down.

So next time there's an uncontested scrum or a
perplexing penalty at the breakdown and you don't
know why, hopefully Barnesy – and a few friends
– can help. Subscribe for more rugby nerd videos
at https://www.youtube.com/@WayneBarnesRef